Devour
Art & Lit Canada

AF255866

Devour:

Art & Lit Canada

is dedicated to the Canadian voice.

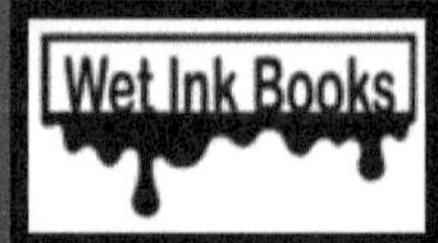

www.WetInkBooks.com
ISBN – 978-1-989786-97-0
ISSN – 2561-1321
Issue 018

Devour
Art & Lit Canada

Find some of Canada's
finest authors, photographers and artists
featured in every issue.

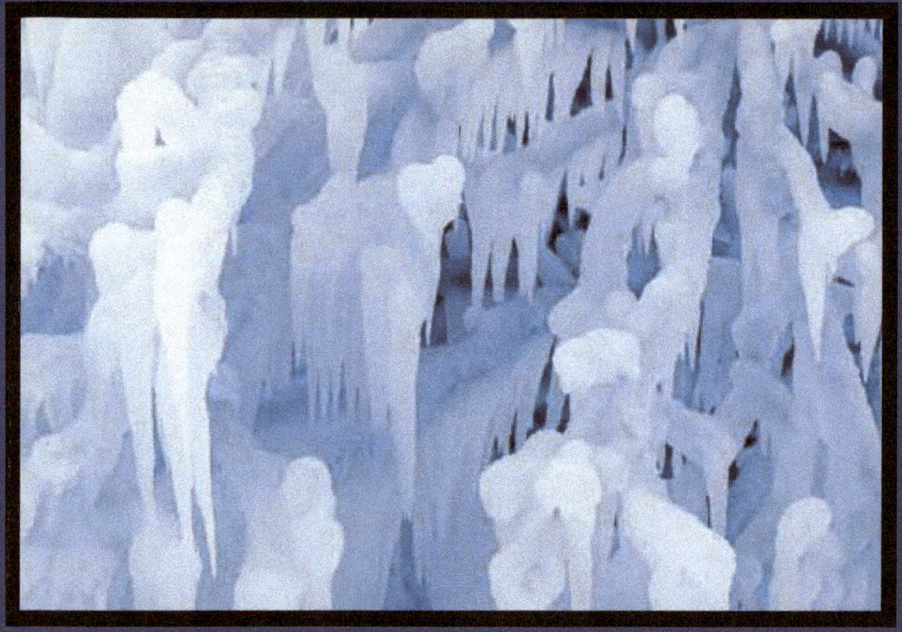

Jason Pettit
Front Cover Image

The mission of *Devour:*
Art and Lit Canada

is to promote Canadian culture by
bringing world-wide readers some of our best
Canadian literature, art and photography.

Devour: Art and Lit Canada
ISSN – 2561-1321 – digital
ISBN – 978-1-989786-97-0 – paper back
Issue 018 Winter 2023 / 24

5 Greystone Walk Drive
Unit 408, Toronto, Ontario, Canada, M1K 5J5
DevourArtAndLitCanada@gmail.com

Editors and Curators:
    Poetry Editor – Bruce Kauffman
    Review Editor – Shane Joseph
    Indigenous Curator – Debora Puricelli
    Photography Curator – Mike Gaudaur
    Prose Curator – Brian Moore

Editor-in-Chief – Richard M. Grove
Layout and Design – Richard M. Grove

Welcome to this 18th issue of *Devour: Art & Lit Canada*. As usual we are bringing you some of Canada's most talented prose writers, poets and photographers. We hope you will tell your international readers about this all Canadian cultural magazine. We are pleased to introduce our new Prose Curator – Brian Moore – with his short story and his first chosen Prose Feature – Lois Hibbert. Stay tuned for what Brian will have for us in future issues. Welcome back Mike Gaudaur with your Feature Photographer – Jason Pettit and welcome back Debora Puricelli with your Indigenous Photographer – Robin Sutherland. There is always a special thank you to our main stay Editors, Bruce Kauffman and Shane Joseph – they have been with us from the start. Thank you all Editors and Readers.

See you between the pages.
Richard M. Grove otherwise known to friends as Tai

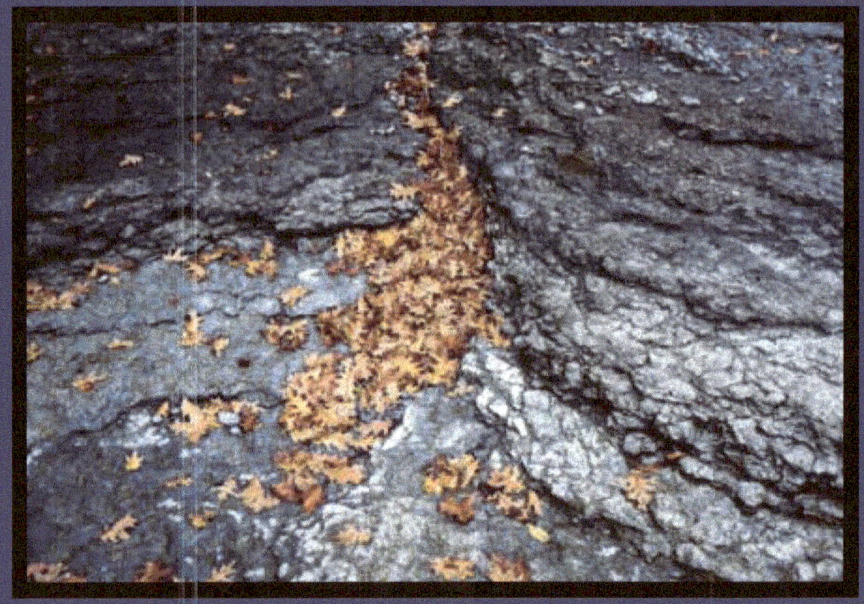

Jason Pettit

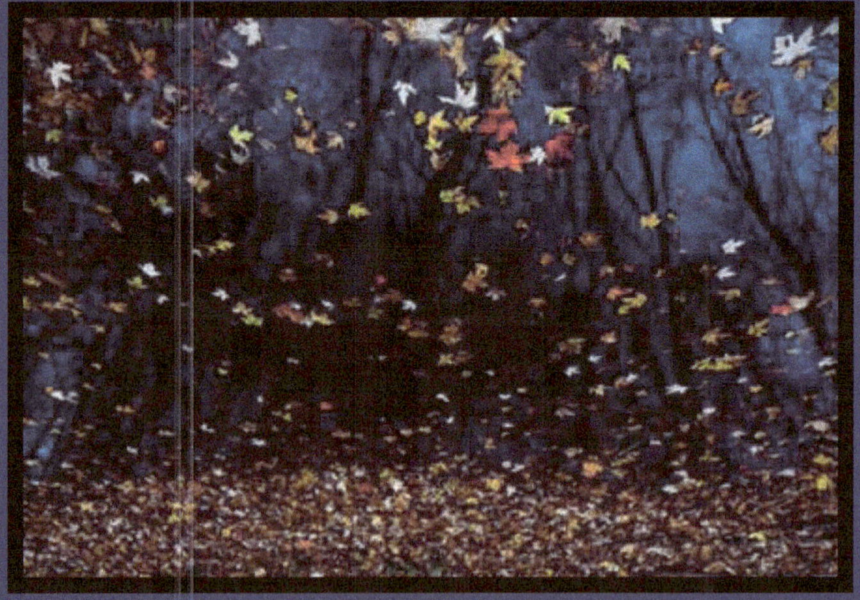

Devour
Art& Lit Canada

Content

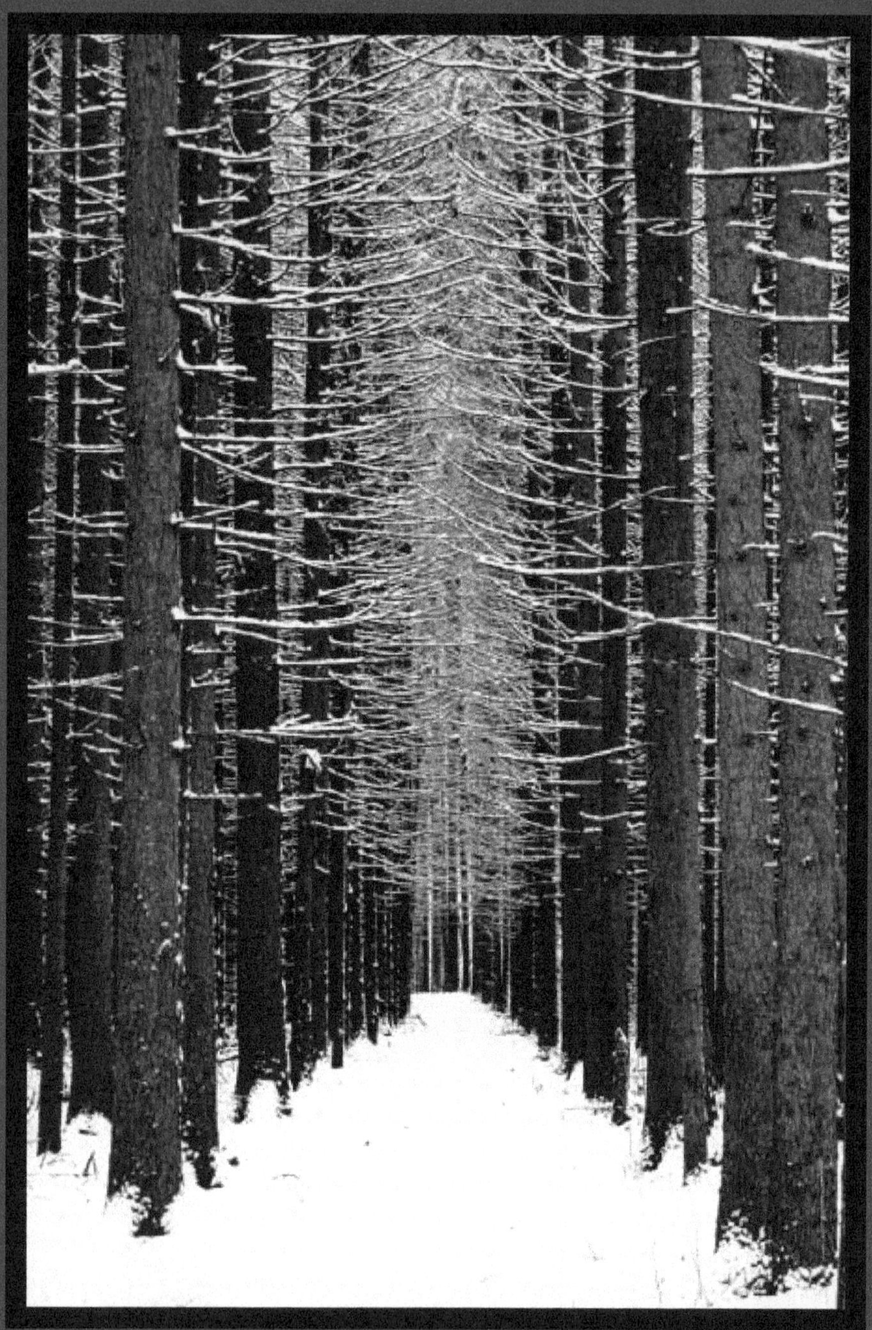

Jason Pettit

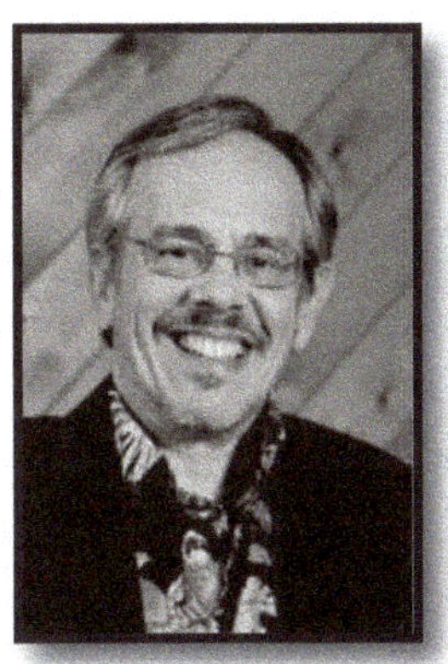

Book Editor's Note:

In this winter issue, and following the recent fall releases of many Canadian publications, we have a bumper crop of book reviews on a wide range of topics for your reading pleasure. I wish I could include them all, but due to space constraints, I have picked seven reviews of six books to whet your appetite sufficiently and make you curl up by the fire with one or all of them during the cold days ahead.

Reality merges with fiction in Kathryn Kuitenbrouwer's autofiction, *Wait Softly Brother*. Beverley Brewer takes things a step further into the real world of family tragedies—four, in fact— in her masterful memoir, *Dance into the Light*, a journey of survival through illness, loss, and suicide. John B. Lee talks of his growing up in *A School Called Normal* where the lessons he learned have held him in good stead to this day. We travel to Vietnam and to a world of secrets that were only declassified a few years ago in Janice Barret's debut novel, *Authorized Cruelty;* and nearer to home, Janet Trull entertains us with a lovable cast of characters, including a ghost, to shed light on the founding of the town of Haliburton in *End of the Line*.

We reserved the "end of the line" of our reviews to feature a double-header: two reviews, one by a poet and the other by a novelist, of *the same book*, a collection of poetry, *Everchild*, by Gwynn Scheltema. This face-off has long been on my agenda, for I have often wondered how a poet would view a work compared to a prose writer. I hope this twin review helps to broaden our interrogation of literature. Perhaps in a future issue we could have a poet and a novelist review the same novel?

I hope you enjoy this collection of reviews, and I wish you all the best for 2024.

Shane Joseph

Title: *Wait Softly Brother*

Author: **Kathryn Kuitenbrouwer**

Publisher: **Buckrider Books**

ISBN: 9781989496664

Number of Pages: 242

Published Year: 2023

Reviewed by **Shane Joseph**

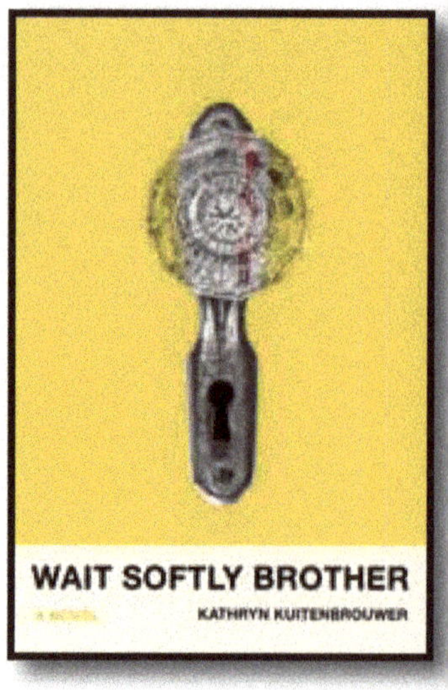

This novel, or autofiction, is a remarkable entwining of story strands — one contemporary, the other historical, in alternating chapters — to render the message that relationships humans put asunder, human nature will strive to reunite.

In the contemporary strand, Kathryn, the author, is obsessed with uncovering what happened to her older brother, Wulf, who died soon after his birth, or so she's been told. She still sees his ghost in the forest. But how does one uncover a story of an infant who did not live long enough to record one? The attempt to write Wulf's narrative drives Kathryn to face her dissatisfaction in life, abandon her 25-year marriage and teenage children, and return to her parents' home in rural Ontario which is under siege from rising floodwaters. Sifting through six generations of family memorabilia, she stumbles upon the record of her great-great-grandfather, Russel Boyt, a substitute soldier in the American Civil War. In lieu of Wulf, she pursues Russel.

Russel's story is a fictionalized one which Kathryn constructs from traces of diaries and letters found in the flooding basement. This tale is far more interesting with the number of bizarre plot twists it involves. Russel is a reflection of Kathryn's mental state — when there is no record, she makes something up. He is a runaway like her. He falls in love with a colored free slave, fights horrible battles in the war, loses a limb, and kills the one he loves. He pleads insanity and enters an asylum.

Kathryn is battling her parents: her mother who is in the throes of dementia yet willing to drop hidden secrets with perfect recall; her father, who is the embodiment of the patriarchy "Women don't sweat." Both parents do not wish to reveal the past. They want Kathryn to suck it up and return to her family before the road washes out. And Kathryn escapes after they are flooded in, to go to America to collect information on her errant ancestor, and get back to the waterlogged house – ours is not to question how or why, but to enjoy the ride. Unreliable narrator?

Late in the novel, just when I thought that all imaginative pathways had been explored, the twins emerge to take both stories through to their resolution. The stories converge in the final chapter, but I'm not letting on any more. In resolving Russel's story, Kathryn is able to come to accept her own sibling's passing, and we hope, will now return to her nuclear family, although that part is not covered. Perhaps this other reconciliation is in the sequel, which must follow, for there are more concealed, generational records in the flooded basement to auto-fictionalize, I'm sure.

In Kathryn's narrative, the writing is energetic, even frenetic. Her anger with the marital breakup and her disenchantment with the world is palpable. Russel's narration is more apologetic. The alternating chapters between the present and the past, however, was a constant "stop and start" for me and broke dramatic thrust. At a crucial point, Russel's first-person POV becomes insufficient to carry his story and an omniscient narrator (Kathryn) takes over to tell us all that's happening to and around him – novel-craft be damned!

I found this an ingeniously constructed autofiction. One wonders how much is real and how much is fiction, and how many real-life people in the book put up with being cast in an unfavorable light — the acknowledgements section may provide a clue. That's why I feel sorry for those who marry writers — beware, you will be auto-fictionalized, in some shape or form!

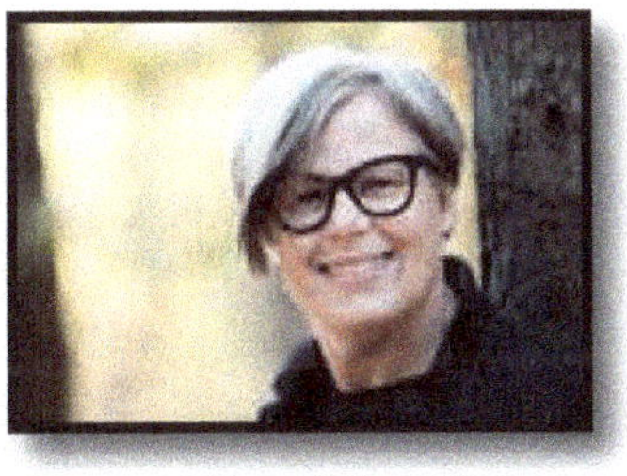

Kathryn Kuitenbrouwer is the author of the novels All The Broken Things, Perfecting, and The Nettle Spinner, as well as, the short fiction collection Way Up. Her recent work is published in Joyland, Numéro Cinq, Significant Objects, Riddle Fence, Filter, The Walrus, and Granta.

She teaches at The University of Toronto and online through The New York Times Knowledge Network, and advises students in the University of Guelph MFA.

Shane Joseph is a Canadian novelist, blogger, reviewer, short story writer, and publisher. He is the author of seven novels and three collections of short stories. His latest novel, Empire in the Sand, was released in the Fall of 2022. For details visit his website at www.shanejoseph.com.

Title: *Dance into the Light*

Author: **Beverley Brewer**

Publisher: **Blue Denim Press**

ISBN: 9781927882832

Number of Pages: 234

Published Year: 2023

Reviewed by **Pam Royl**

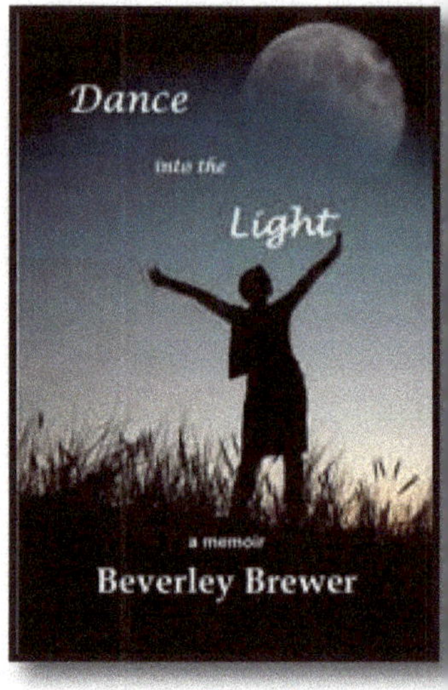

From the very beginning of *Dance into the Light*, we are dropped headlong into the grief, disbelief and guilt surrounding the suicide of a loved one. In vivid detail we experience the author's discovery of her dead sister, Jacquelin, and learn that Brewer's husband, Jack, is in cancer treatment, her father has just been placed in long term care, and her mother has recently passed away. This memoir tells a story of a life in crisis and of the strength and resilience of the author to find a way through.

Told in compelling, creative non-fiction style this memoir is hard to put down—until the weight of the story is too difficult to witness and we are compelled to take a break—at times one feels as if we are watching a train wreck in slow motion. But the story keeps calling the reader back as we quickly become invested in the author's tortured journey to make sense of why her youngest sister committed suicide; we too must know why an intelligent and beautiful young woman would choose to end her life.

With accomplished literary skill, Brewer shares her struggle to help Jacquelin deal with alcoholism and its destructive force. Trying to piece the reasons together, Brewer ponders whether undiagnosed mental illness might have played a role in her sister's death and delves into their shared childhood, searching for insight.

This is a deeply personal story of Brewer's journey through grief and guilt, driven by the hope of reclaiming herself. In the first few pages, she writes, "I have thought deeply about my sister's challenges and the reasons for her final choice. I have also pondered our relationship and how impossible I found it to extricate myself from her life. Before she died, when I inserted my presence back into her unyielding and chaotic life—mostly uninvited—I found myself standing on uncertain ground. I wanted to rescue her, but I didn't expect to abandon myself. The seven-year struggle was immense. In my person journals I grasped at hints of light in the despair surrounding my youngest sister's suicide."

One theme that shines throughout this gripping story is the devoted relationship she has with her husband, Jack. He supports his wife with informed guidance and compassionate help during her sister's tortured downward spiral. The fact that he did so while undergoing cancer treatment is astounding. One gets the sense of an unbreakable bond between these two people, so much so that they can get through anything.

The narrative moves effortlessly back and forth in time as fragments of Jacquelin's life are sown together by agile writing to find resolution to the unanswerable question of "Why?" and the guilt of "Why couldn't I save her?" We become emersed in Brewer's desperate and sometimes misguided quest to save her sister, in the midst of coping with the aching need to help her husband through debilitating cancer treatment, and her failing father through the difficult transition to living in long term care. The epilogue, which she refers to as "Lessons in the Light" inspires hope for those who have a family member or friend in crisis—and for everyone who believes that a better understanding might possibly result in lives saved.

It must have taken tremendous courage to write this deeply personal and revealing memoire. It is strongly recommended for readers who seek inspiration from the resilient capacity of Brewer to rise above crushing adversity to help those she loves, even if it means losing, and then finding, herself along the way.

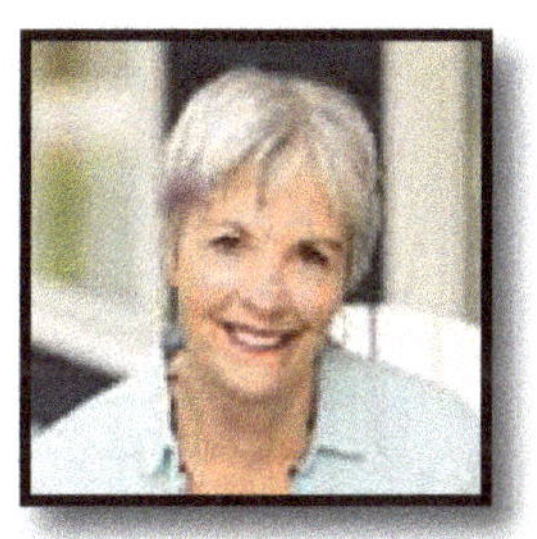

Beverley Brewer's training in life skills teaching methodology set the stage for her life's work. She completed her PhD at the University of Toronto. Following an award-winning adult education career Bev plays at singing, kayaking, hiking and writing fiction and memoir. Bev is a member of the Muskoka Authors Association and lives in Muskoka with her husband and two black labs.

Pam Royl was inspired to write her debut novel, The Last Secret, by an ancestor she discovered while writing family memoirs. Developing her fiction writing skills through courses at the University of Toronto, and the mentorship of International award-winning author, Donna Morrissey, Pam set her story within the fascinating history of Northumberland County, where she lives with her husband, Ian.

Title: *A School Called Normal: Poems and Stories*

Author: **John B. Lee**

Publisher: **Mosaic Press**

ISBN: 9781771617086

Number of Pages: 140

Published Year: 2023

Reviewed by **Patrick Connors**

Normal schools were institutions designed to train teachers. The trainees were children in primary grades and high school, not university graduates. As such, these young people could expect to be subjected to discipline.

"The Superintendent" is one of the authority figures we are introduced to by Lee. She came to the classroom one day per term to preserve a sense of order, and to let everyone know who had the final word in that order. But even the narrator, who carved their own name into a desk, seems to realize the need for such correction: "for we are the bullied, the shy/the wild, the plump/the brilliant, the lost/the bratty, the eager-to-please." Presumably, some of these traits would have to be unlearned in order to teach the generation following.

"In the Evening of My Youth," almost in the centre of the book, begins with the peak of adolescent hormones, "...the sexy ululation of words/libidinous verbs/and lascivious nouns/watching the walk-away/in the hem sway like soft bells/of the short-skirt girls."

From there, the narrator recounts the assassinations of Robert F. Kennedy and Dr. Martin Luther King Jr. The following stanzas recall an industrial fire in Windsor, Ontario, the Mai Lai massacre, and other events filtered through the lens of the six o'clock news.

The final stanza is an exquisite denouement from all this rising action: "...the snow/came down veiling/the light at the barn/like what you might see/in the glow of a ghost/or the breath of an angel/were you not sleeping the sleep of the young."

This is an example of moving from the personal to the universal, from the banality of our limited individual scope to the larger problems of the world, and then back again. What makes it work so well is the concluding stanza.

"I Don't Remember the Moonlight but I Do Remember the River" is one of the best titles I have ever seen for a poem. The narrator is caught up in a despair which is beyond adolescent angst. "in early October of my youth/there on the dreary banks of the Thames/at the edge of an audible flowing/feeling only mostly the emptiness of life."

The sixties were a time of great promise and freedom, and the reality of the world's ugliness intruded on that freedom and led to disillusionment. But here we see a timeless existential crisis which can happen to anyone at any time, with all the requisite choices to be made. "I had become lost in the blank sadness/of a sorrowless mind/well beyond woeful/wishing more to never have been - more/*this* than to cease to exist/to be unfound and forever unfindable."

This book argues that too much freedom, and not enough of the discipline and focus from the Normal School years, led to the state that the world and the author were at during this time. Being beyond sadness, being unable to feel or care, is the worst of all.

John B. Lee had a head of massive curly hair in those formative years, and still listens to rock and roll. However, the discipline he gained at Normal School was necessary to focus the considerable acuity required to inform and create his formidable body of work.

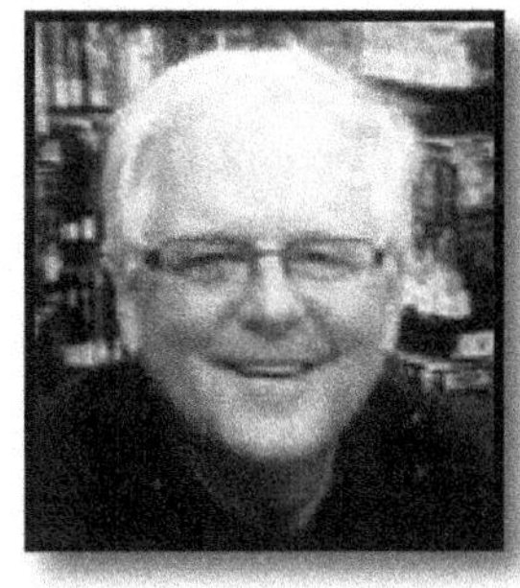

John B. Lee is a recipient of over eighty international awards for his writing. He has more than seventy books published to date and is the editor of twenty anthologies. His work has appeared in excess of 500 international publications. Called "the greatest living poet in English" John lives in a lake house overlooking Long Point in Port Dover, Ontario.

Patrick Connors' first chapbook, Scarborough Songs, was released by Lyricalmyrical Press in 2013, and charted on the Toronto Poetry Map. His first full collection, The Other Life, was released in 2021 by Mosaic Press. His new chapbook, Worth the Wait, was released in 2023 by Cactus Press.

Title: *Authorized Cruelty*

Author: **Janice Barrett**

Publisher: **Blue Denim Press**

ISBN: 9781927882917

Number of Pages: 220

Published Year: 2023

Reviewed by **Gail M. Murray**

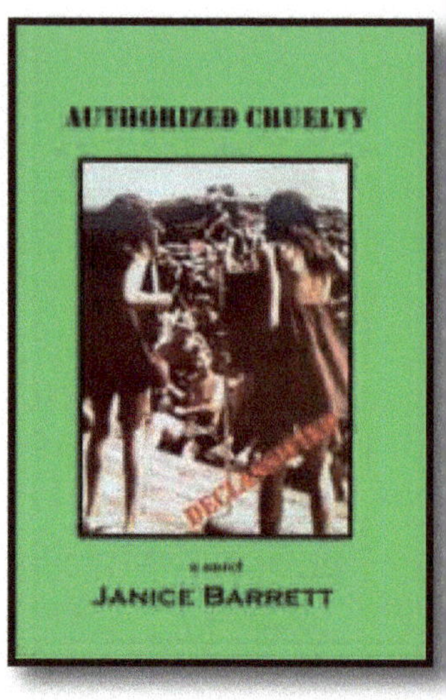

In her debut novel, Barrett's impeccable research, in particular Matthew Connelly's *The Declassification Engine* and Daniel Ellsberg's *The Pentagon Papers*, transports us to 1968 Vietnam – the worst year of the conflict. This was the time of Bobby Kennedy's and Martin Luther King's assassinations, Kent State student beatings, and protest marches for civil rights and Women's' Liberation. Barrett creates a feisty heroine in twenty-four-year-old, anti-war protester and USO entertainer, Patty Fielding. Barrett's mother, a professional dancer, was about to entertain the troops in WWII when a broken ankle prevented her contribution.

Why a novel set in Vietnam? At fourteen, Barrett saw her cousin return from that country a changed person. What happened to change him so drastically? This question also propels Patty's concern for her brother Christopher in Da Nang when he writes "you can lose who you are here; there's no normal."

Inhumanity and desensitization, a recurring theme, is captured many times in the novel but especially when the author describes Christopher. "Suddenly he was tired of being numb, and afraid to feel, tired of seeing corpses bagged, tagged, and shipped to become nothing more than inconvenient paperwork."

The soldiers' Zippo lighters used to light flame throwers to burn and destroy villages became symbols of destruction and inhumanity.

After performing for the camp, Patty pays a visit to the field hospital, moving from bed to bed, singing for the wounded soldiers, holding a hand, brushing a cheek – little acts of kindness. "She offered comfort to these men. To give them a piece of home to hang onto "...she saw in their faces that her touch made a difference. It somehow added humanity that was missing."

Barrett wisely gives the reader moments of quiet beauty before the intensity ensues. One moment that stands out is the scene between Patty and the young lieutenant, Pete, relaxing at an idyllic waterfall. Pow. Suddenly he's hit by a sniper. Dead. Patty returns to camp to find nothing left but dead bodies, the survivors retreating after a major assault (the Tet Offensive), and her fellow entertainer evacuated by helicopter to safety.

Patty sets off alone through the jungle, facing dangers from land mines, patrolling Vietcong, ravenous ants, mosquitos, poisonous snakes, and cutting elephant grass. We breathe easy when she encounters an encampment of American soldiers. Not so fast. They don't want her. She could thwart their secret mission. Here she's privy to crude remarks, chauvinism, misogyny, manhandling, sexual harassment, and attempted rape. One heroic soul emerges from the jungle locker room bravado: Soko, short for Sokolowski, to become her protector.

Barrett's descriptions are visceral. There is non-stop, edge-of-your-seat action, constant obstacles, and attitude to overcome in this vivid action adventure.

Although Patty is a general's daughter who felt close to her father on the shooting range, she hates the army where orders supersede decency and common sense. Politicians and generals often viewed the war from opposing positions; President Kennedy warned: "beware the generals." Barrett flushes this out creatively in her novel.

Even when the mission is accomplished and the operatives are flown back to the States, something is amiss. Is Patty safe in her own country? The generals see her as a threat. Full of intrigue, action and rife with political undertones, the author uses fiction to bring this war home.

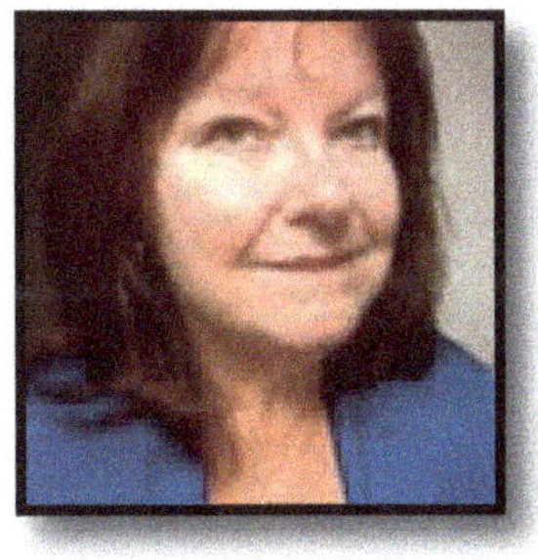

Janice Barrett is a mother of three. Her children are her proudest accomplishments. She is a journalist, playwright and ghost writer. She gave a seminar at The Niagara Falls Literary Festival in 2018 on "How to Write a Memoir." She spoke at Canada's Coast to Coast Tenacious Women's Literary Series at the Laura Secord Homestead.

Like Keats, **Gail M. Murray** seeks to capture the essence of the moment. Her writing is a response to her natural and emotional environment. Discover Gail's poems in Written Tenfold, *Blank Spaces, Wordscape, Arborealis, and The Banister. Find her* creative non-fiction in *The Globe and Mail,* Devour, *Trellis, Heartbeats, Renaissance, NOW Magazine, Blank Spaces*, and *Our Canada.* Her debut collection of poetry, Reflections & Reveries, has just been released.

Title: *End of the Line*

Author: **Janet Trull**

Publisher: **Blue Denim Press**

ISBN: 9781738914500

Number of Pages: 260

Published Year: 2023

Reviewed by **Liz Torlée**

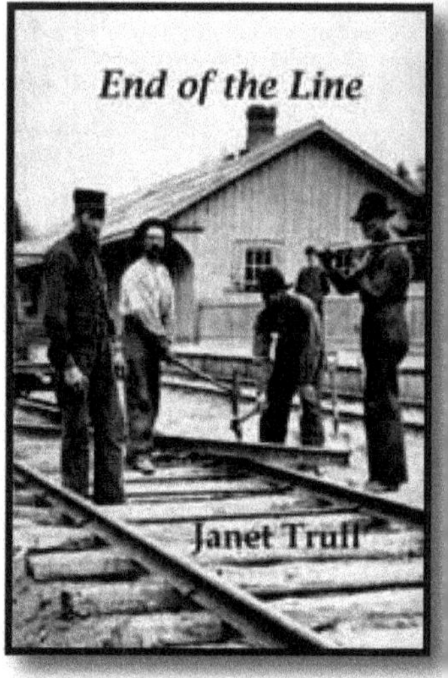

Where to begin? Well, how about an enigmatic ghost who clearly knows what's going on in the neighbourhood, and a couple of dead bodies whom nobody seems too upset about. But, lest anyone think this might be a murder mystery, think again. *End of the Line* is highly entertaining fictional tale about the challenges, secret pleasures and general shenanigans of the community of Haliburton at the end of the Victoria Rail Line in the 1880s.

With her amazing and enviable skill at both description and dialogue, Trull brings an extensive cast of characters to life and makes us care about all of them … well, almost all. It is difficult to pinpoint the principle protagonist, but the story is rooted in the life and beliefs of the compassionate but tough as nails Winona (*"call me Ona"*) McLeod, who inherited land and established The Nunnery, a refuge for *"women from society's tattered margins."* Ona is a pagan at heart with deep respect for nature, but no one messes with this woman who *"does as she pleases, smokes a pipe and drinks whiskey like a man."* We become immersed in the daily lives of citizens Ona keeps a cautious eye on … bank manager, shopkeeper, housekeeper, care giver, handyman, sawmill owner, spinster schoolteachers, undertaker, and many, many more, as well as their wives, husbands, and children beyond count.

We learn quickly that some men in this community are far from upstanding — either lazy with little ambition, or plenty of ambition and no conscience. Particularly reprehensible are Alex Smith, the much detested, mean spirited bank manager, and the hapless Reverend Whitlock, a man with distinctly un-Christian proclivities, including *"opium laced tonics"* from the nearby gypsy encampment. As the author puts it: *"Men of degraded morals find each other and commit their atrocities in the warm glow of each other's approval."* These two degenerates form a distinctly unholy alliance with devasting consequences.

It is, however, the women who propel the story along. They turn a deaf ear and a blind eye to the failings of their husbands, and, on the surface, seem to accept their subservient roles One of the women is left a widow with twelve children to raise, one is committed to an asylum for controversial treatment, another is left to bring up her child by a married man … and there are many more sad tales. Ona herself was abandoned by her mother. These women do housework, farm work, and men's work, with little complaint. This was the way of their world. But if any of them was in trouble or seriously abused, they would close ranks and become a formidable force, and this force is the thread that weaves through the whole novel.

I did get a little lost sometimes with the sheer number of characters, their names, occupations and who was related to whom, and I felt the odd person — Ona's mother, for example, who appears and disappears rather abruptly — could have been scrapped with little impact on the thrust of the narrative. But the delicious building of tension and the sheer beauty of the writing were so engaging that it was easy to gloss over this.

The curiosity sparked by the deaths and "whodunit" in the opening pages is eventually rewarded, and I closed the book delighted with the conclusion and disappointed that it was over. *End of the Line* was a sheer joy to read.

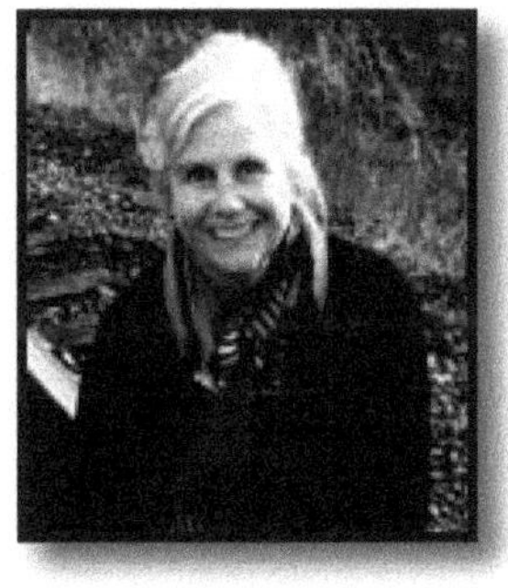

Janet Trull is the author of two critically acclaimed collections of short fiction, Hot Town and Something's Burning, published by At Bay Press and available worldwide. Her essays and award-winning stories have appeared in the Globe and Mail, Toronto Star, Canadian Living Magazine, Prairie Fire, The New Quarterly, subTerrain Magazine, and Geist, among others.

Liz Torlée lived and worked in England and Germany before emigrating to Canada. She has always been fascinated by the idea of fate and the way it makes all our lives intersect in strange and far-reaching ways. She and her husband are avid travellers, especially through the Middle East … or any country with a desert! They live in mid-town Toronto. In Love with the Night is Liz's second novel.

Title: *Everchild*

Author: **Gwynn Scheltema**

Publisher: **Aolus House**

ISBN: 9781738914500

Number of Pages: 100

Published Year: 2023

Two Reviews

The Poet's Review (Antony Di Nardo)

Of Moongates and Toads:

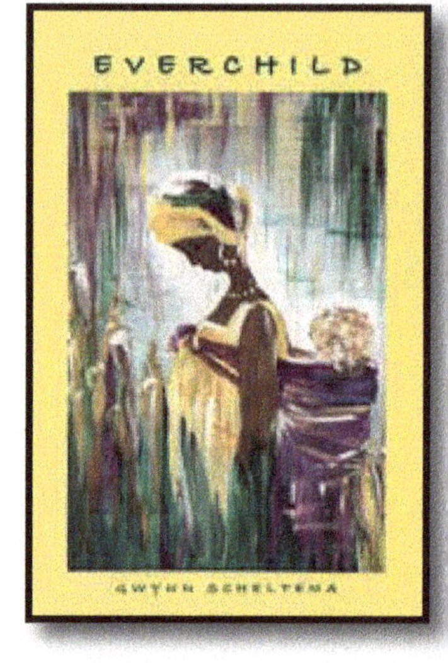

Poetry comes from many places, different sources, bundled in a variety of shapes and sizes, highs and lows. Some retreat into shadows, others rub against the light and catch fire. Poetry offers the reader a peek into the heady wanderings of the heart or a sideways glance towards a world of possibilities where poems are swings, badly tied Nikes, a cottage deck. Boarding passes. A stone-cold toad. Moon gates.

"Moongate Prophecies," the poem that prefaces Gwynn Scheltema's new collection of poetry, *Everchild*, locates the reader at the brink of such far-ranging possibilities and begins

> *where the forest path begins,*
> *two arching trees*
> *touch — form a moon gate*
> *over stones*

We are about to step into that liminal space between landscapes and interiors, waking and dreaming, immersed in the experience of poetry where anything can happen when you put your mind to it. The poem continues:

<blockquote>kneeling, she feels the flow of mind
to finger bone turning
arranging, rearranging
her prophesy of stones—</blockquote>

What else but language can give rise to prophecy? To music like this? What else but "the flow of mind" can dictate hands to rearrange the world we know into poetry? Words are "stones" that "gather light," words that contrast the inner-outer values of the poetic experience. And if you roll these words in your mouth you can feel the sumptuous syncopation of the long i's and long o's in the soundscape they announce before the final stanza concludes the poet's *ars poetica*:

<blockquote>in salutation arms wide
she breathes in deep
treads lightly
on what was
what will be—</blockquote>

The poet steps through the "moon gate" relying "on what was" to bring about "what will be"—experience transformed (translated, actually) by the art of poetry into broken lines, and "never to be found again / in quite the same way," as we're told in her next poem, "The Old Swing," where the reader hears "the creaks and jangles / clank of chains" in a poet's voice.

Scheltema's poetry also demonstrates what words can do when they dredge up memories, sketch a moment between two people, or pick at scabs of bloodied feelings. This can be dangerous ground for a poet where the risk of sentimentality can overwhelm and run a poem off the rails. It shows up when she writes about motherly love or its absence ("Patience" and "Mis/Placed"), but it's rescued in poems like "Elissa," about a newborn baby. We read that "In time // such newness will age." Time, after all, is the lifeblood of so many of these poems.

In *Everchild*, we find poetry that is both clear-headed and clarifying, poetry that both describes experience and creates it. Scheltema pays meticulous attention to the sounds and pictures within words and knows which ones best belong. Her poet's palette is both varied and far-reaching – she can bring Molly Malone back to life as well as take us into the heartland of Zimbabwe.

There's a lifetime in these poems and in that lifetime, stories to be told about people, places, the state of the human heart, whether grieving or skipping to the beat of its own music. She writes: "I am bonded to a long dynasty of toads / fighting ever to hold my tongue"– thankfully, it's a losing battle and she speaks volumes, enchanting us with images such as "light and heart and mind drain like bathwater / through the back of the canvas."

Everchild by Gwynn Scheltema-Anderson has much inside its pages to make us think about the side effects of reading poetry. I enter a world I've been a stranger to up till now. "I could not name what made me cry" is the final line of *Regina Septemvittata*, a poem about a snake that mesmerizes the poet and casts a spell— *uncoiled, unslinked.* The poet, like the snake, slips into these poems and takes us with her.

The Novelist's Review (Shane Joseph)

Everchild is autobiographical, of someone who inhabits two worlds: Southern Africa and Canada, not unlike the worlds I have inhabited as an immigrant. It's a splintered world that we will try all our lives to bring into focus as one, but will only end up with a collage of fragmented images that make for an enhanced view by the reader, but an incomplete one for the writer.

The book comes in four parts: Breath, Ignite, Ebb, and Be, with poems grouped under them, not so much for chronological progression but to indicate moods. Through these groupings emerge powerful imagery.

"Breath" dwells on a childhood of nannies more caring than mothers, wild animals, *kukuyu* grass, a marriage broken when she was six, a mother who never embraced and said "I love you," the wicked stepmother who took Mother's place, of singing Molly Malone while driving with a father who never talked about the war.

In "Ignite" the young woman is aroused to passion:

> *If I had time, I'd bring you breakfast on a silver tray,*
> *stretching and arching against the day's*
> *duties lined up outside the door*
> *my nipples peak*
> *and I snuggle into sheets.*

Only to be abandoned in the poem "I am Rain":

> *…you called for me once, longed for me, needed me*
> *but now you follow the sun.*
> *Rain is not welcome on evening walks…*

The harsh life-lessons continue in "Ebb":
"Your father said to tell you he's not your father," – Stepmother.
Mother finally gives her a hug after scolding her thoroughly for various childhood shortcomings.
"There are toads in my family…toxic secretions spit from my mouth" – the realization of family heredity. "You say I am my mother."
And the final announcement of release from a 25-year marriage, in a letter to Mother: "I left him today, I know what you told me. I made my bed, and lie in it I did."

The poet finds resolution in the final part, "Be." It is a time of remembrance, of how cows were milked back home; of letting go of a father and mother who pass, Father to be remembered fondly for all the times they shared, and Mother to have this book dedicated to. A time of aging and remembering the bi-polar world of the immigrant where similar things look different: Naartjies in Zimbabwe and their equivalent Oranges in Canada, for instance. A time of meeting old friends who have made similar immigrant journeys and who make this not such a lonely path. And of frequent visits to the toilet at night, thankfully shared with one's spouse, again not making it a solitary journey:

> *And I finish up and stumble back, still*
> *in the dark, meet you outside the bathroom door*
> *Pass the baton, you say. My turn to pee.*

Peering out in places are derivative poems based on paintings or poetry created by others. There are references to a mysterious K who "lost her way" to ALS, and to the drowning of a three-year old, not elaborated on in the helpful Notes section that give the reader context. Perhaps these revelations are for another time, another collection. But all is not gloom, for "Elissa" is a tribute to the poet's eldest granddaughter:

> *sucking at air with her round bow mouth,*
> *a heart so fresh and small,*
> *it has no room for sorrow.*

This collection is bold in a vibrant African way and circumscribed in a polite Canadian way, reflecting Scheltema's artistic journey as well as her immigrant one.

African Moon Moth (*Argema Mimosae*)

That day a yellow-gold leaf fluttered
on my child-palm, pin thin legs tingling my skin,
long leaf stem tail dangling
the fold and furl of her, her furry
fringes like blown dust,
warmth grew in my chest.
I wanted to keep her close, to wonder
at her again and again in small pieces, a little each day.
Can I keep her I asked.
No you said.
She will live only a few days.
She doesn't have a mouth. She cannot eat.
She has her own purpose, and you must not keep her from it.
As if on cue, she opened her wings, red eye spots seeing me
for an intimate instant—and left me.
Like my mother.

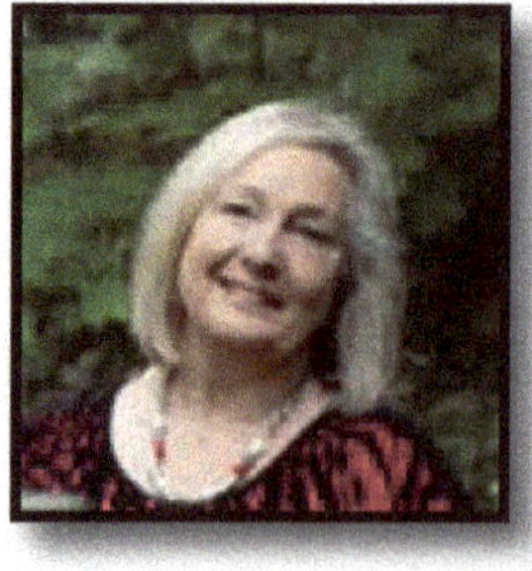

Gwynn Scheltema is published in anthologies, journals, and magazines in Canada, Europe, and South Africa, online and in print. Her poetry chapbook, Ten of Diamonds, was published in 2021. She is the president of Northumberland Festival of the Arts, and co-host of Word on the Hills on Northumberland 89.7 FM. Her website is www.writescape.ca.

Antony Di Nardo has written seven books of poetry. His work appears widely in journals and anthologies across Canada and internationally, and has been translated into German and Italian. His long poem suite "May June July" was winner of the Gwendolyn MacEwen Poetry Prize for 2017 and was short-listed for a National Magazine Award. His book, Through Yonder Window Breaks, won the inaugural Don Gutterson Poetry Award. He spent the last years of a teaching career in Beirut where he launched his first book of poetry Alien, Correspondent in 2010. He is an active member of the League of Canadian Poets and the Cobourg Poetry Workshop.

Shane Joseph is a Canadian novelist, blogger, reviewer, short story writer, and publisher. He is the author of seven novels and three collections of short stories. His latest novel, Empire in the Sand, was released in the Fall of 2022. For details visit his website at www.shanejoseph.com

Heart Song

Whimpers wend like wind spirals
from the child swaddled on her back who whispers
with spirits she does not want to know
a mother gone that no-one speaks of
thula, thula, hush hush

this child hums alone in shadows stirred
by tree song and unseen shifts of air
thula, thula, hush hush

safe now, a black arm slipped beneath
her small body they walk the mile
to the orchard in shared warmth
steady steps in heart-rhythm music
beyond words untying knotted nerves
calming evermoving fingers and toes
thula, thula, hush hush
ngilapha, I am here

in slanted afternoon light
syringa trees hang heavy
with wax white blossoms
and poisonous pearl berries
alien in this acacia savanna
"Speak English only to her" they say
She sings an Ndebele lullaby
thula baba, thula sana
"Don't take her beyond the garden" they order
she climbs the hill to gate 6
passes into the orange orchard where citrus scents
slow a troubled heart
in that cool resting place in the dark shade
releases the cotton wrap
swings the toddler in a practiced arc from her back
removes the sandals with brass buckles
removes the dress with itchy white lace
gathers her to her breast
skin to skin
white to black
thula, thula, hush hush
ngilapha, I am here

by Gwynn Scheltema

Canada Coast to Coast to Coast

Photography Curator
Mike Gaudaur

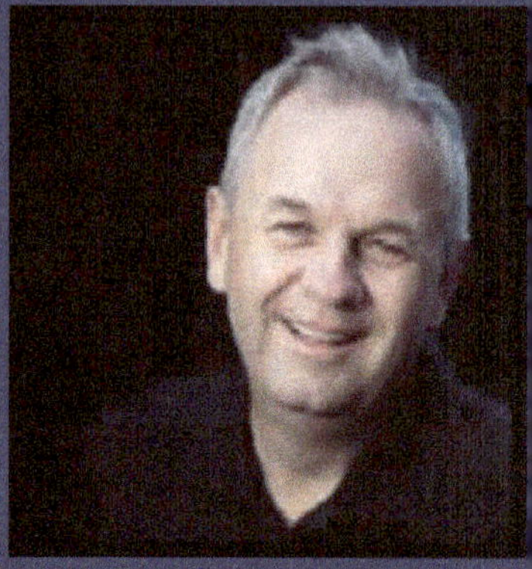

Before submerging himself into photography as a career he trained as a teacher. Throughout college and his first ten years of teaching he continued to shoot weddings, portraits, and sports. It was only after taking a teaching position in Kenya that wildlife and landscape photography became his passion.

He continues telling about his path into being a professional photographer by telling me that: "Teaching photography provided me with lots of opportunities to photograph, develop, and print; to

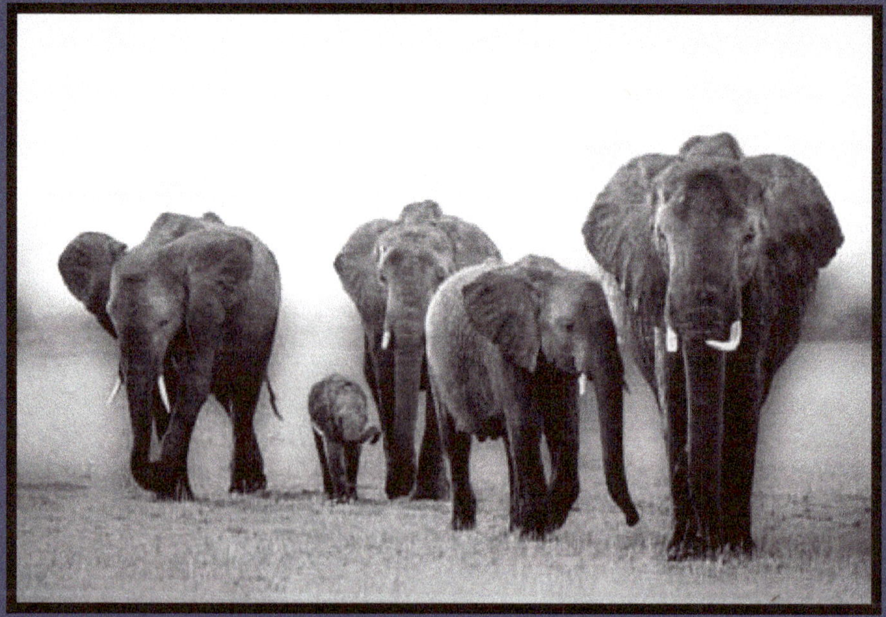

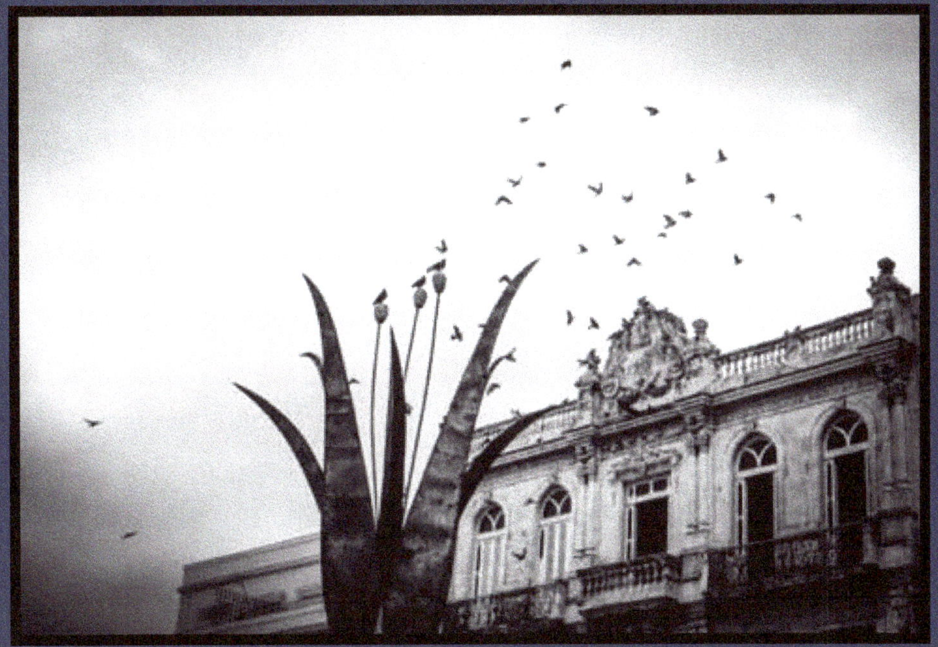

refine my 'craft and vision.' The school's switch to digital photography seemed inevitable so I began to research and learn all I could about the new digital world. Digital capture and processing enthralled me, but it was not until inkjet printing came of age that I was willing to commit to a totally digital workflow."

Mike has spent the past 12 years teaching photography during school terms and photographing on safari during the term breaks. Online training and countless late nights of experimenting resulted in Mike developing a full complement of digital skills. After returning to Canada he was able to formalize his training and become an Adobe Certified Expert in Photoshop. Mike is a never ending learner, experimenter, explorer. His learning didn't stop with Photoshop. He naturally grew into working with Lightroom, On 1 Perfect Photo Suite, and the Nik Software collection. His advanced skills in the digital technology have allowed him to push his photographic style even further.

You can find mike at: https://www.mikegaudaurphotography.com/

or contact him by email at, mike.gaudaur@gmail.com

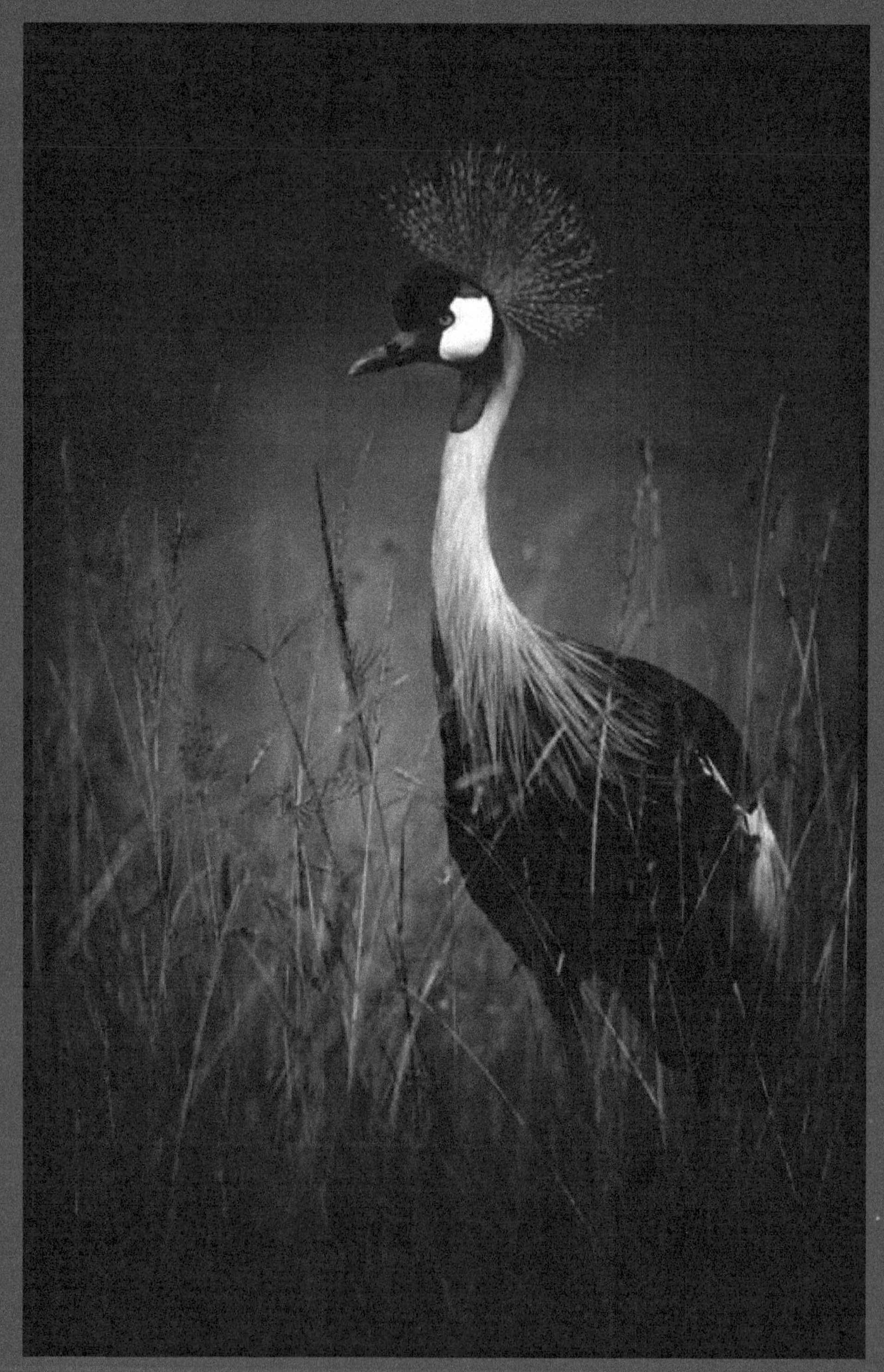

Mike Gaudaur

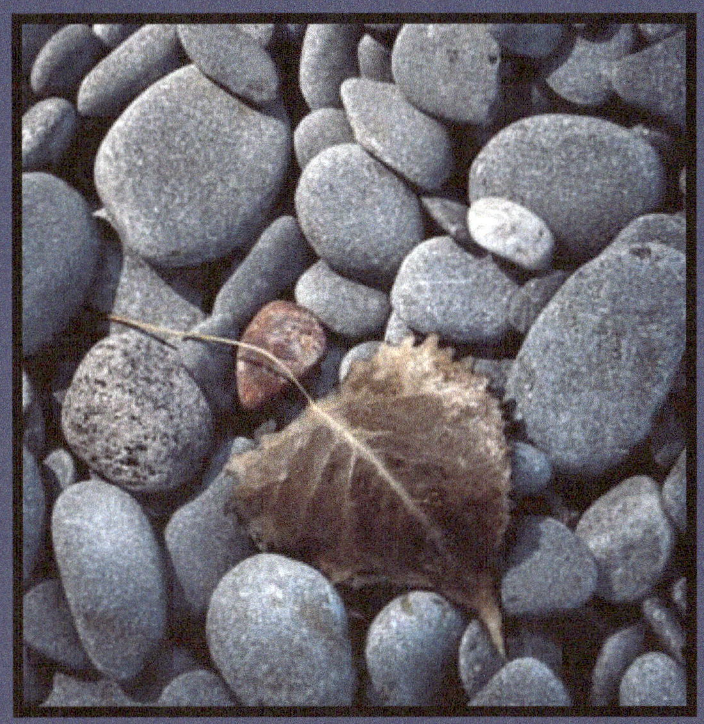

Mike Gaudaur

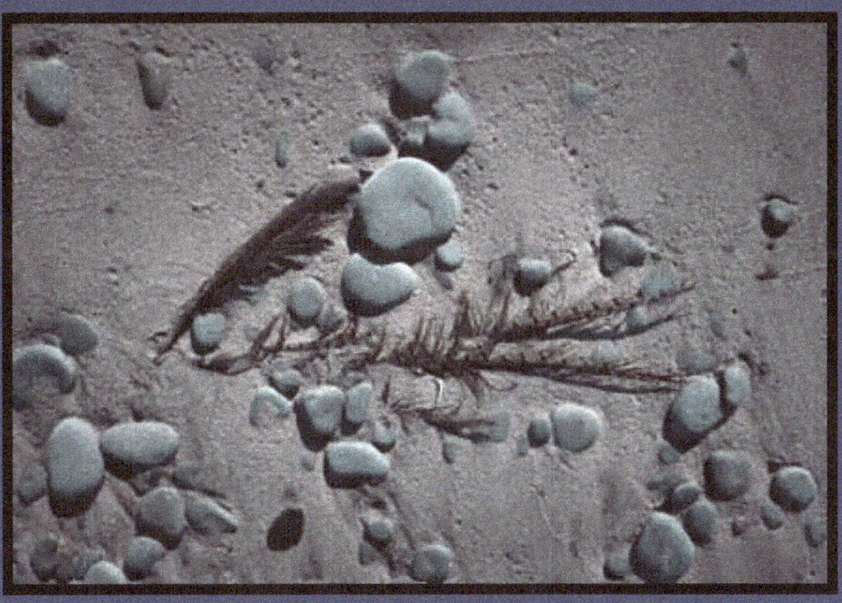

Jason Pettit is a man of few words.

"I'm an artist working in the photographic medium residing in Prince Edward County, Ontario, Canada."

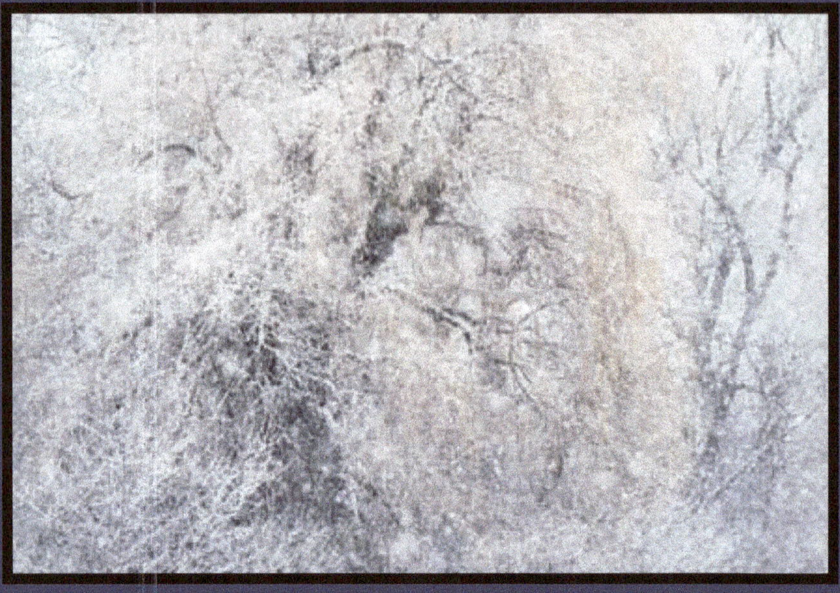

Jason Pettit

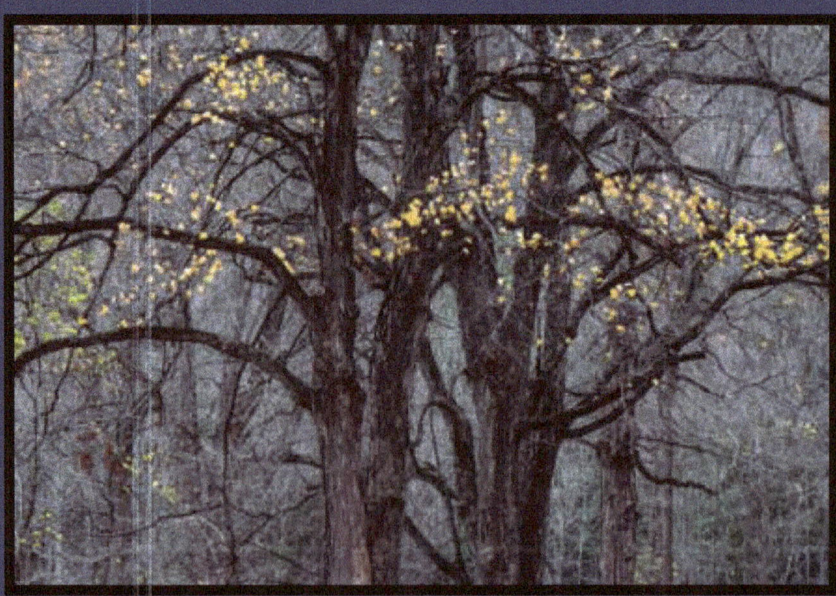

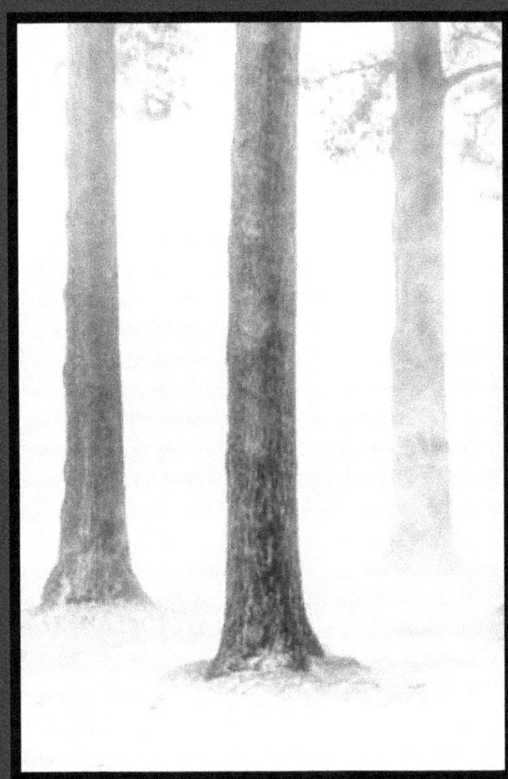

Jason Pettit

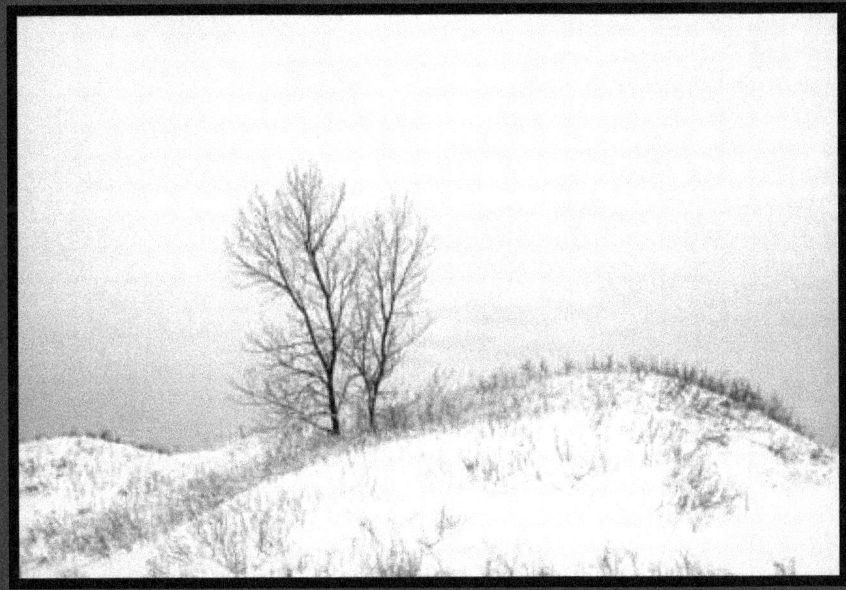

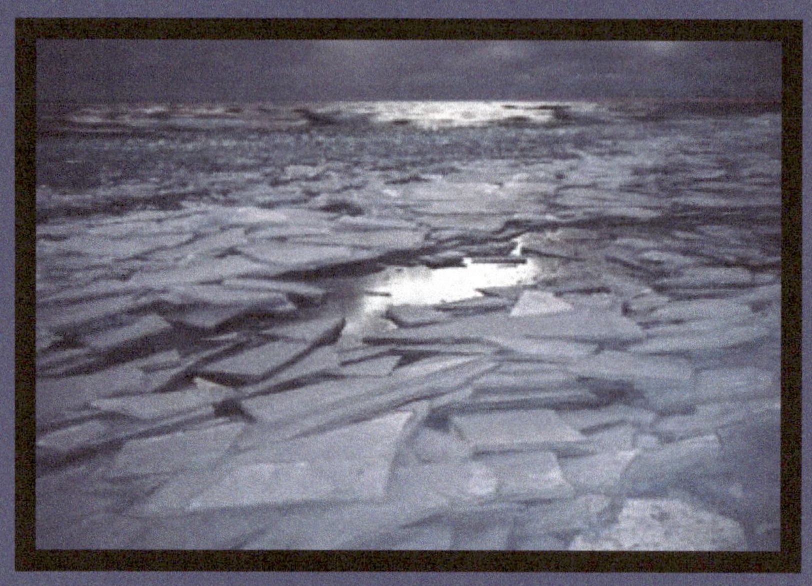

Jason Pettit

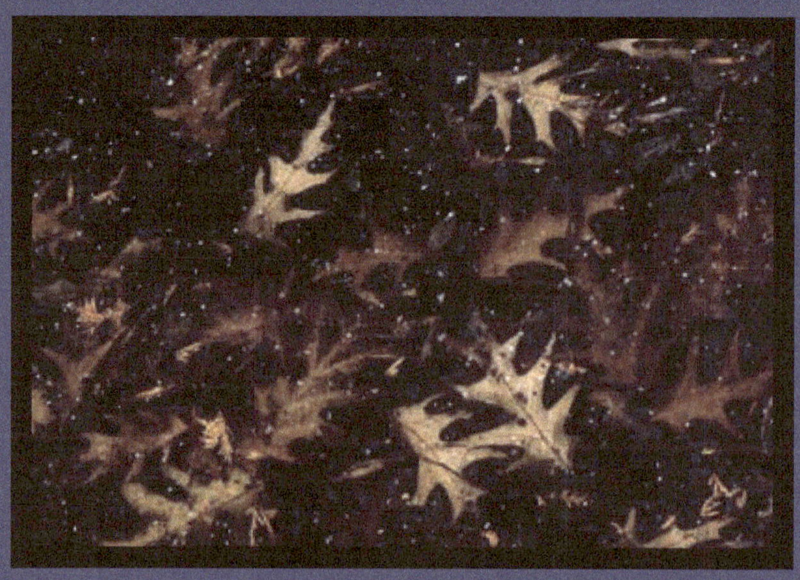

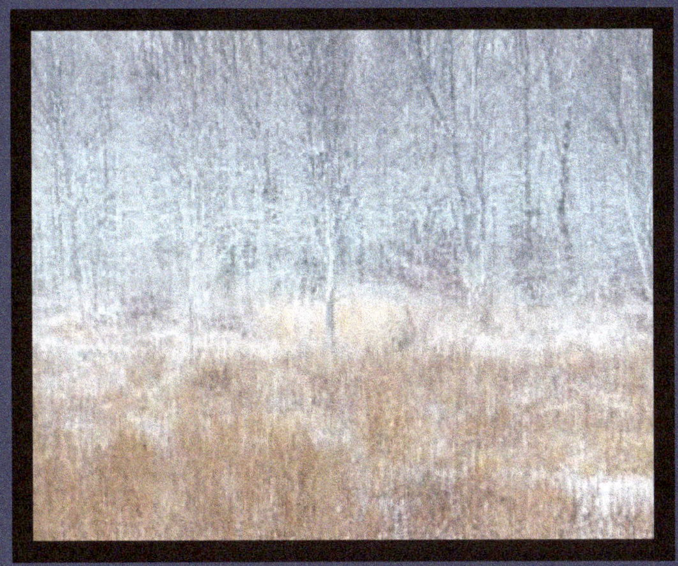

Jason Pettit

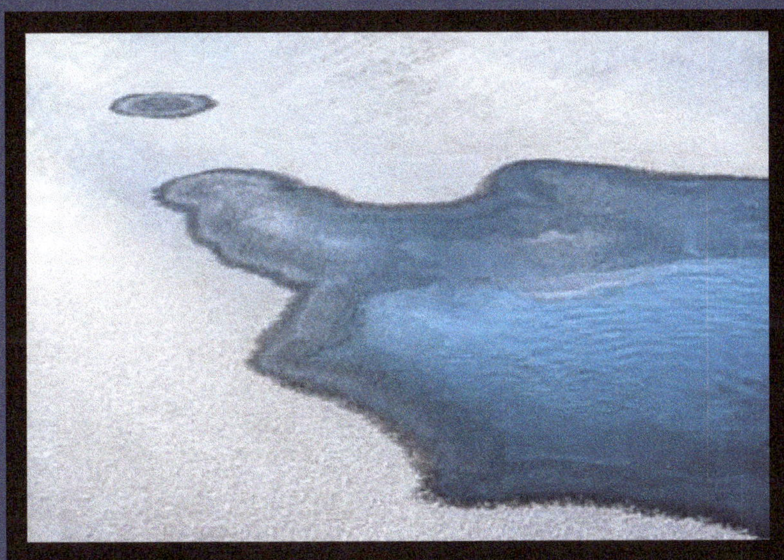

Poetry Canada

Poetry Editor: Bruce Kauffman
Photo Editor: Richard M. Grove

Bruce Kauffman
"Poetry Canada" Editor

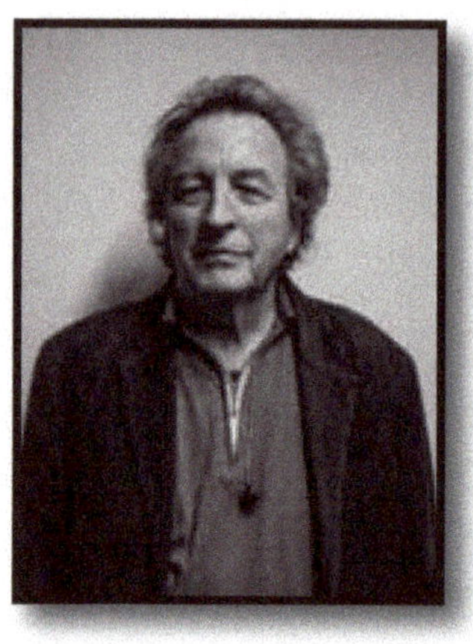

Bruce Kauffman lives in Kingston and is a poet and editor. His latest collection of poetry, an evening's absence still waiting for moon, was published in 2019. He facilitates intuitive writing workshops, and hosts the monthly and the journey continues open mic reading series begun in 2009, and also produces & hosts the weekly spoken word radio show, finding a voice, on CFRC 101.9fm he began in 2010.

once

once there was
      a day
      or a moment
      or a person
      a thing
so brilliant
so perfect
it could never
      happen again

and then it did

pattern

keenly aware –
the patterns of the clouds
this morning
exactly the same as
they always are
      17 hours before it rains

and in this hour –
birds singing
fervent squirrels
         gathering
insects all moving
           scrambling
in each their own language
of day

how the leaves hang
     differently

how shadow reveals
     a lighter shade

how you will see that
     city fox
come out from hiding
earlier   then later
the one you hadn't seen
in weeks

there are so many worlds
in this one
so many days rolling inside
this hour

sometimes   i forget
     to watch

     to listen

Bruce Kauffman
bruce.kauffman@hotmail.com
Kingston, Ontario

light

there is a light
      under a ledge

it goes nowhere
it remains
to perhaps highlight
      perhaps direct

the colour it throws is
a pale, watercolour blue

i do not believe it was
designed that way

i believe the light
has instead chosen that colour

its choice
to illuminate
      as if day
and to imitate
      the sky

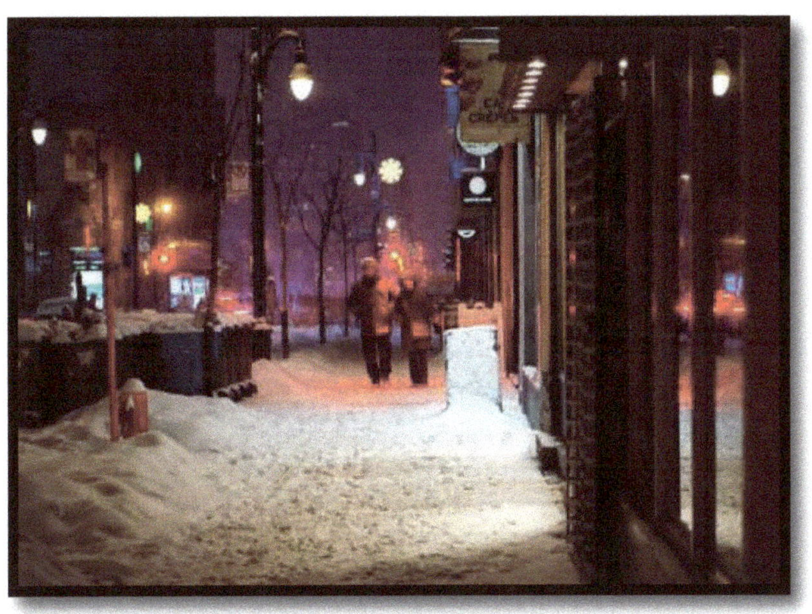

Rick Waldau, Montreal Winter Streets
Instagram Photorick2022

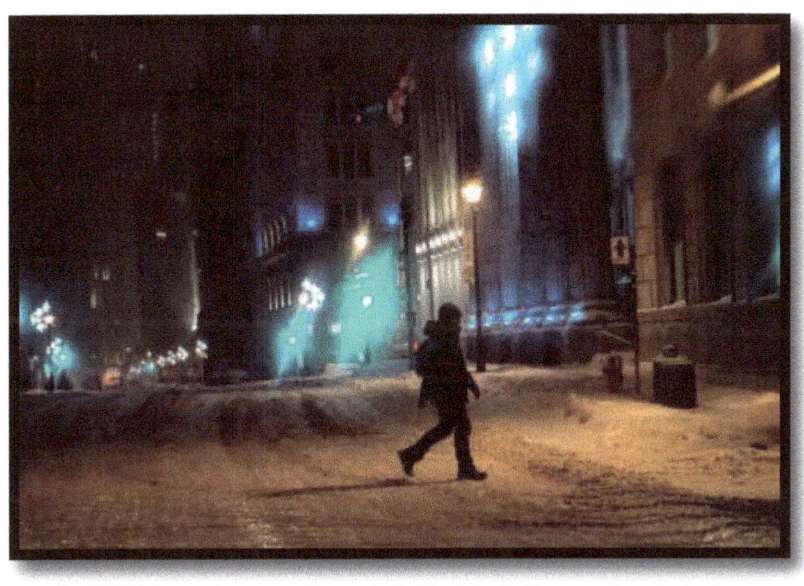

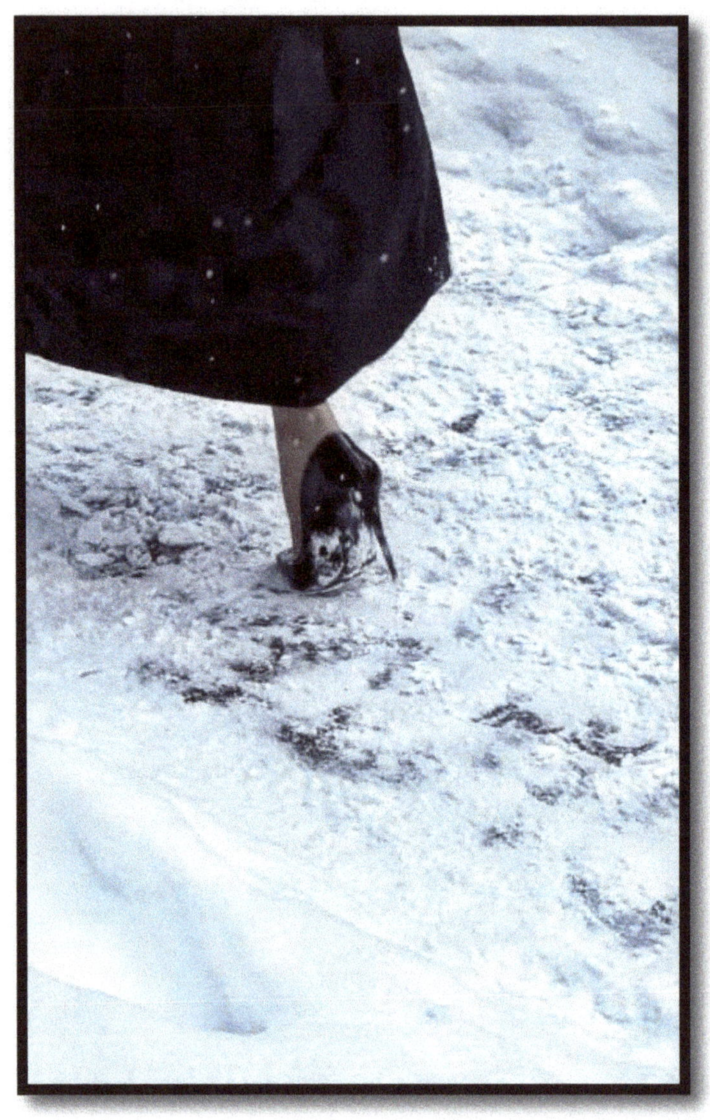

Rick Waldau, Montreal Winter Streets
Instagram Photorick2022

International Amateur Street Photography Group Winning Pic

A. F. Moritz
albert.moritz@utoronto.ca
Toronto, Ontario

The Gift

I've long given up the dream
of having something to do
with the coming of the good kingdom.
Just let it be coming and let me live
over to one side
and then when it arrives let me live
in one of its rooms off one of its alleys.
It will be plenty simply finally
not to fear my own filth, the puzzle
of the whereabouts of food, the rain
of muddy plaster spheres always falling
a little late, mirroring beneath my ceiling
the pure rain after it starts hitting
the porous tar above. It will be plenty
not to meet, whenever I go out, the random
knives into my eye on the sidewalks,
the random onset of blindness, the lying
waiting to be scraped up. Plenty
not to feel the noise of the sirens
screeching nearer as relief. It will be plenty
and undeserved just to be alone
and the least known beneficiary.

Alanna Veitch
alanna.veitch.av@gmail.com
Kingston, Ontario

ascent

there is beauty – peace –
in unexpected things
in an image
focusing upward
ascending and blurred
while   in some way clear
it captures a moment
I was unaware

Allan Briesmaster
abriesmaster@outlook.com
Thornhill, Ontario

Flight of Breath

Without the means to shake encirclement
in my own and the world's grey dust, I'll choke.
… Inhale, exhale. How does one circumvent?
By thought, by feel, stroke after moted stroke

I seek a separate egress, taking breath
through passages branched from an unblocked source
that won't let musty clutter, boding death,
dispirit like the burden of a curse.

The deep dayspring toward aerial energy
eludes the scope of hazy New Age lore.
No magus can dismiss its mystery,
nor savant pinpoint the primordial core.

Aspiring to break stasis and pull free,
I unmoor for a wider way to be:
across that inland sea on windswept shore
where walls blow down between the "me" and "thee."

Antony Di Nardo
dinardoa@mac.com
Cobourg, Ontario

Telemann

And there at her seat by the aisle of St. Mary's
between the flutes and vaulted ceilings

a stranger was dying. I saw her head collapse
and hit the pew like fallen fruit. Stunned,

I shied away and slipped into a thought of
what it would be like to fade that way

under the ballast of the late baroque, brass
and woodwinds sinking slowly into oblivion,

the void of silence that followed before concert-
goers raised their cells and tapped in 9-1-1—

              the *thunk* of her skull,
of its bone-struck beat, still fresh in my mind,

both hands clutching the program
           as if a life depended on it.

Cassie McCoy-Bullock
cassieattrent@gmail.com
Gananoque Ontario

Sink

Let's create more moments we sink into
forget the stable ground
it will return
sink with me
laugh
and forget why you're laughing
let our smiles infect one another
so much that we forget where the feelings begin and end
let's not ask why
I know
it feels important
to keep an eye on time
so it doesn't run away
without us
but let's slip under the canopy together
and forget the world outside it
imagine
this a dream
and you've been given the key to stay
the only way to not wake up
is surrender.

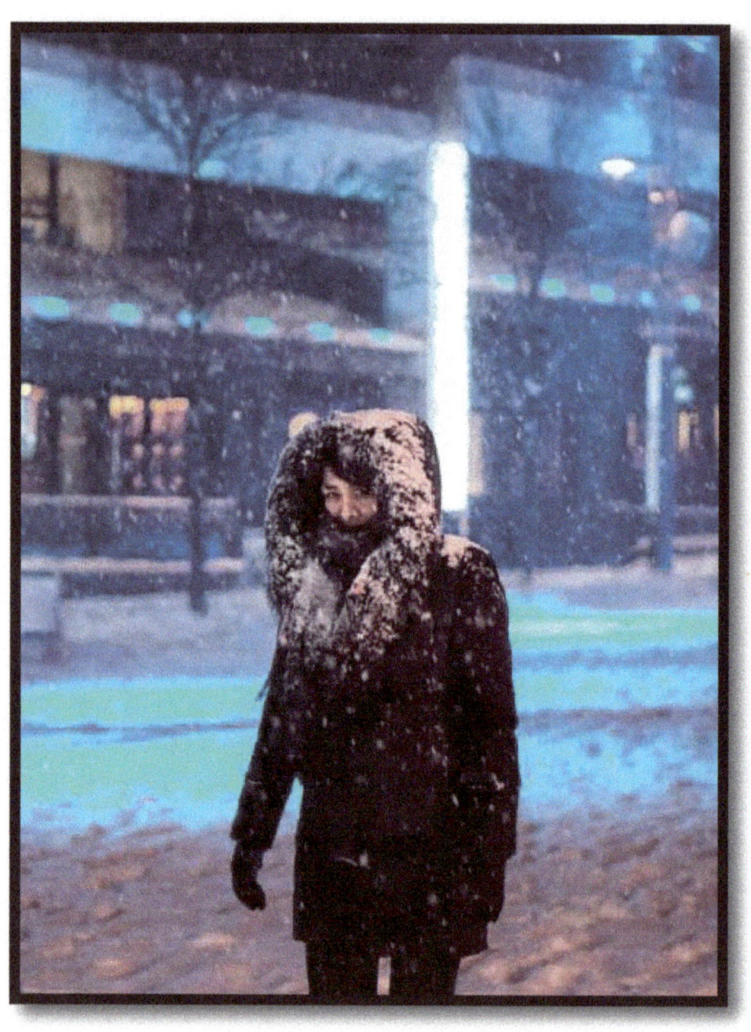

Rick Waldau, Montreal Winter Streets
Instagram Photorick2022

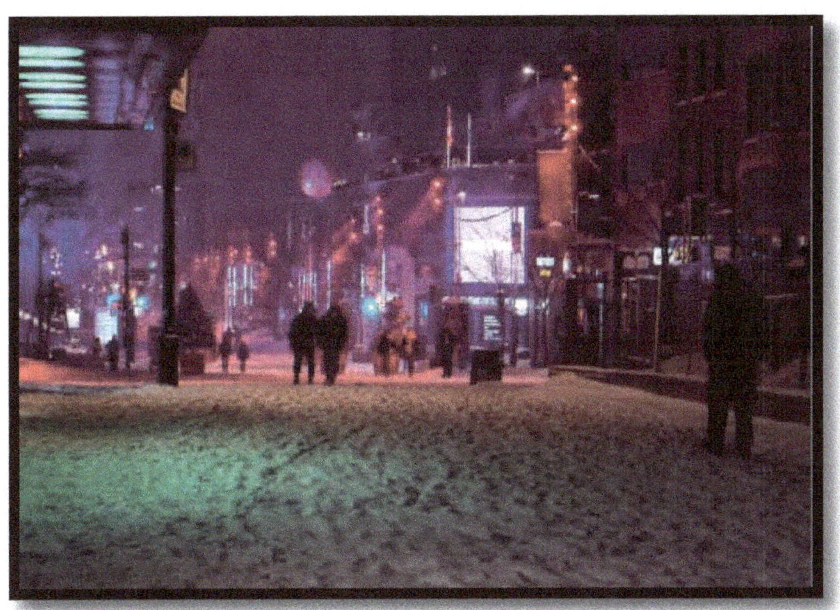

Rick Waldau, Montreal Winter Streets
Instagram Photorick2022

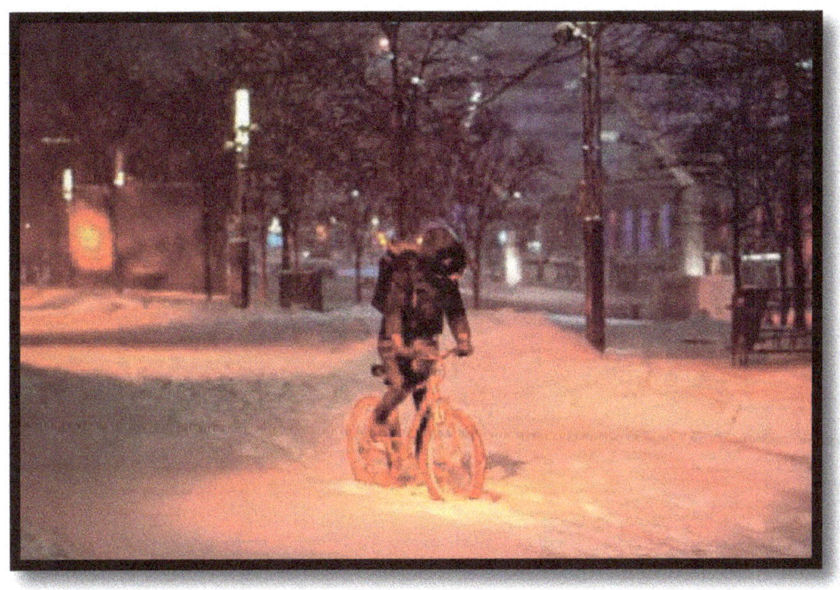

D. Le Doan
dledoan67@gmail.com
Beaconsfield, Québec

Toddlers

Toddlers are the stars
of the playground. Wherever they go
their caregivers follow and circle around.

As if tethered to them by
binding forces of attraction.

And like the roaming stars, toddlers
constantly toddle or run.

Or rock back and forth on the constellation
of spring riders.

Or climb up the stairs toward the heavens before
shooting down the slides.

And shine and twinkle in their dazzling displays.
And climb up again as if

circulating and pulsating inside each of them
were the unbounded energy
of a burgeoning star.

Glen Sorestad
sorstd@sasktel.net
Saskatoon, SK

Three Graves

My uncle insisted three Indigenous graves
were located on one of his grain fields.
He said they had become difficult to see
after decades of the cycle of cropping,
followed by summer-fallowing, before
re-seeding the most current crop.

As a teen, I cultivated that very field –
sixty-plus acres lying west of the creek
that split the quarter-section into near-halves.
Perched on the tractor seat, I scanned
the field ahead for boulders or obstacles,
or the unexpected appearance of animals.

But I admit I was also determined to locate
the disappeared mounds that marked
the final resting place of three people
we never knew, who died long before
my uncle sowed his first wheat kernels
on land those earlier people knew differently.

Several times I'd stop, dismount, walk
to a spot that appeared, from the tractor,
to possess the imagined contours. Each time,
I climbed back up, and reseated myself,
disappointed. Still, I continued the quest.
In the right light, I was sure, I'd see them.

That was seventy years ago. Those three
graves remain there, where they've been,
unmarked and otherwise unremembered,
unless other family lore sustains them.
My uncle is dead, but those graves live
in my memory. I keep them for us all.

D. V. E. McBride
dayle.mcbride@sympatico.ca
Amherstview, Ontario

A Way Back from Grief

Tuesday morning. The cemetery,
a conduit for letting go.
Granite headstone bears witness
to a life, a love
of exquisite tapestry; threads
resist unravelling.

Her stoic figure gives over
to tears past resolve.
Shimmers of light
left on her cheek like liquid glass
cut elsewhere, deep
into the skin of her soul.

Her grief, carried by the wind
to a higher realm, drifts untethered.
She pulls the aubergine scarf tight
to her thin body, leaving pink peonies
splayed across the grave
like kisses.

John Tyndall
London, Ontario

The Noisy Plover

I wake in the night to the call of the *noisy plover*
and I feel as if I'm in a play, a James Reaney play
a character who believes the bird cries for rain, but
the plover – in French *le pluvier*, in German *der Regenpfeifer*
– feeds and pipes alarm in the darkness as well as the day

I step out of the ice cream factory into sweet sunlight
and the song of the *chattering plover* circles in the sky
no broken wing now to fool a predator, an old actor like me
for if all the world's a stage, 'tis a plovery platform
from the rough earth of home to the fine airs of exaltation

I approach what appears a set of commerce where I can choose
a pharmacy for the drugs I need or a cannabis dispensary
for the drug I want, when I see and hear on gravelly ground
Killdeer!   Killdeer!   Killdeer!   Killdeer!   Killdeer!
directing my soul from one scene to another anyway

John B. Lee
johnb.leejbl@gmail.com
Port Dover, Ontario

What am I to do with a good friend ailing

what comes when the easy divinity of youth
lapses into health loss
and the fecklessness
of an old heart
that dog by the fire
in an ill man's breast
he who is ailing
in the broken-body hours
of an ineluctable
mid-day sloven …

revive and be joyful
no longer
the vacationer's houseplant
wilting in a windowsill
the spirit
takes an inbreath
with a deepening swell
so the soul
fills the hands from within
there where
the prayer lines of a long life
touch together to become
an interlacing
of sacred desires in design
like the tangle of threads
in the underside
of mending
that multi-coloured
interweaving of an unseen beauty

when life's inversion
steps out and into
a grateful darkness
like a surgeon with a stranger's heart

K.V. Skene
kv.skene@gmail.com
Toronto, Ontario

Browsing The Haunted Bookshop

839 Fort St., Victoria, B.C.,

Perhaps it's the dusty mustiness
of second-hand books, or the essence

of desiccated binder's paste and hide glue
that makes my most improbable pilgrimages

seem achievable – even commonplace.
Floor-to-ceiling shelves, stacks, set-asides –

authored by famous/infamous 'best sellers'
of obscure heretical, historic or literary eras,

each with an indeterminant shelf life,
no sell-by date,

multipaged and primed for obligatory perusal
whenever my bibliomania goes rogue –

Beowulf? E. Pauline Johnson's Flint and Feather?
*Kinder-und Hausmärchen durch die Brüder Grimm?**

until closing and it's time to choose
what I want …? What I need …?

what I can afford …
and the proprietor smiles his old, old smile

whilst assessing my latest 'find'
Ah yes! What an excellent choice!

** Children and Household Tales by the Brothers Grimm*

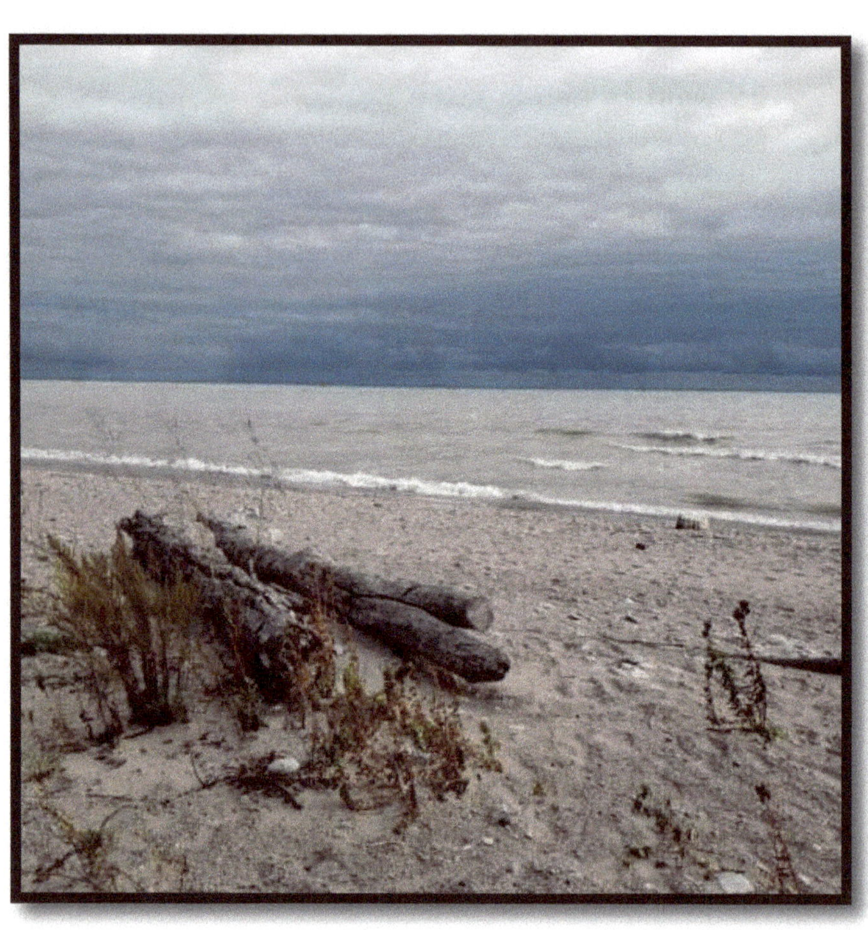

Shane Joseph
Cobourg, West Beach - 02

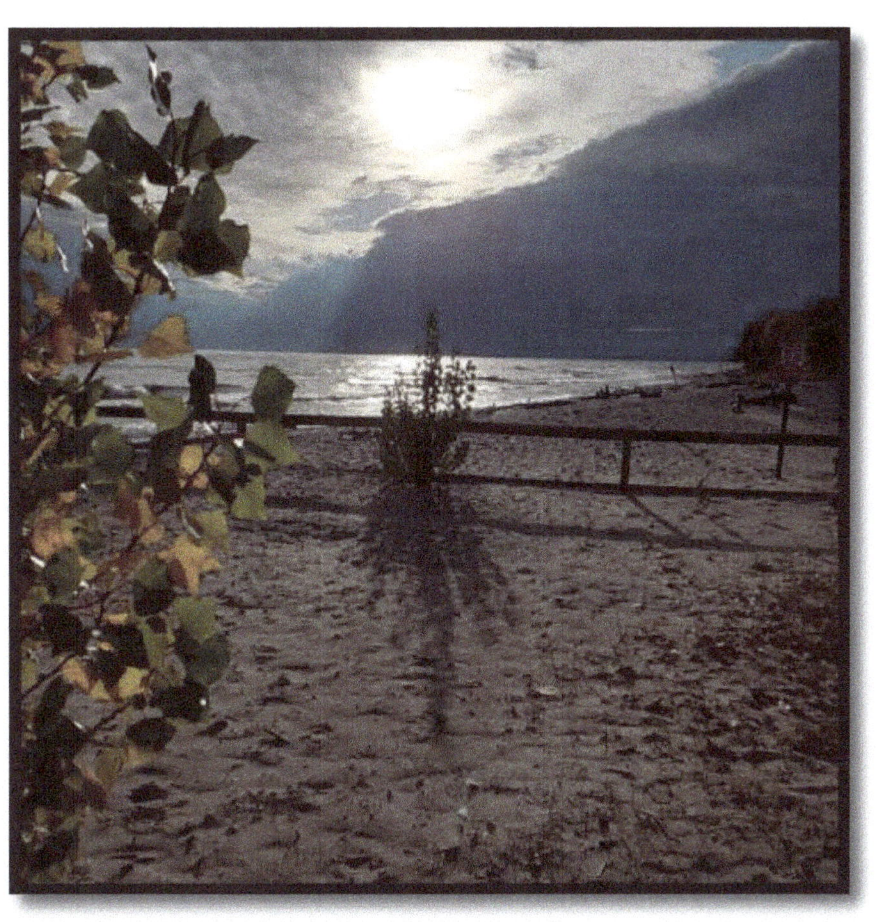

Shane Joseph
Cobourg, West Beach - 01

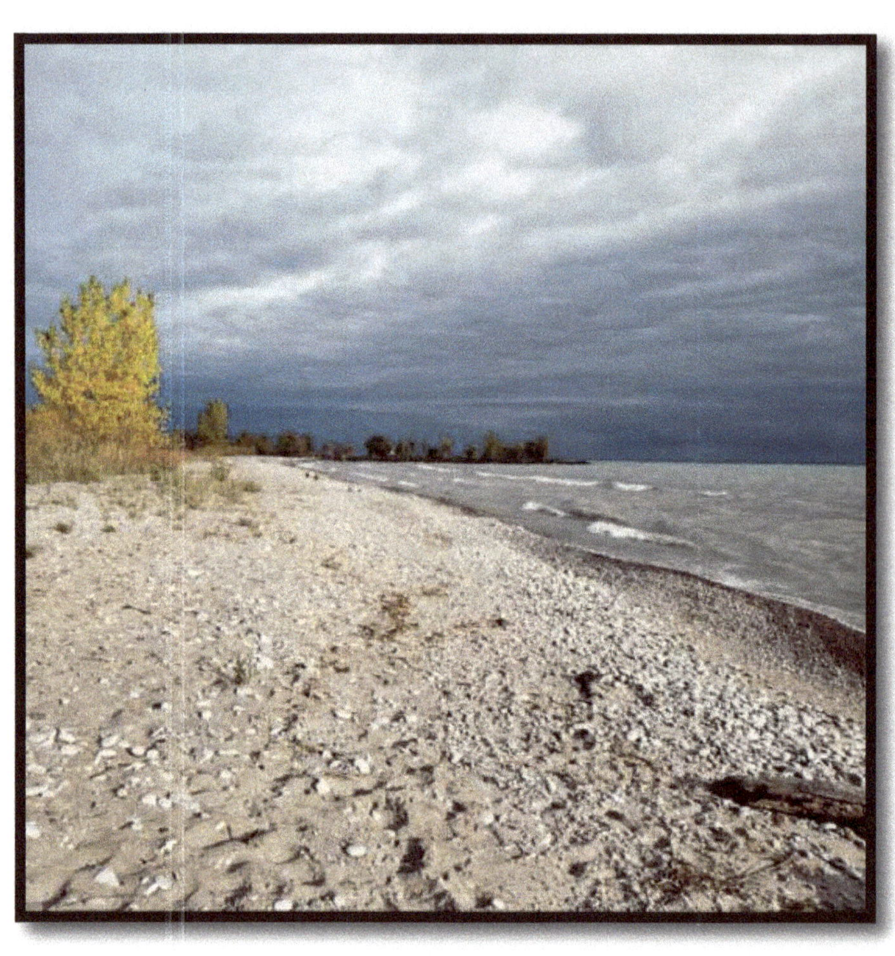

Shane Joseph
Cobourg, West Beach - 02

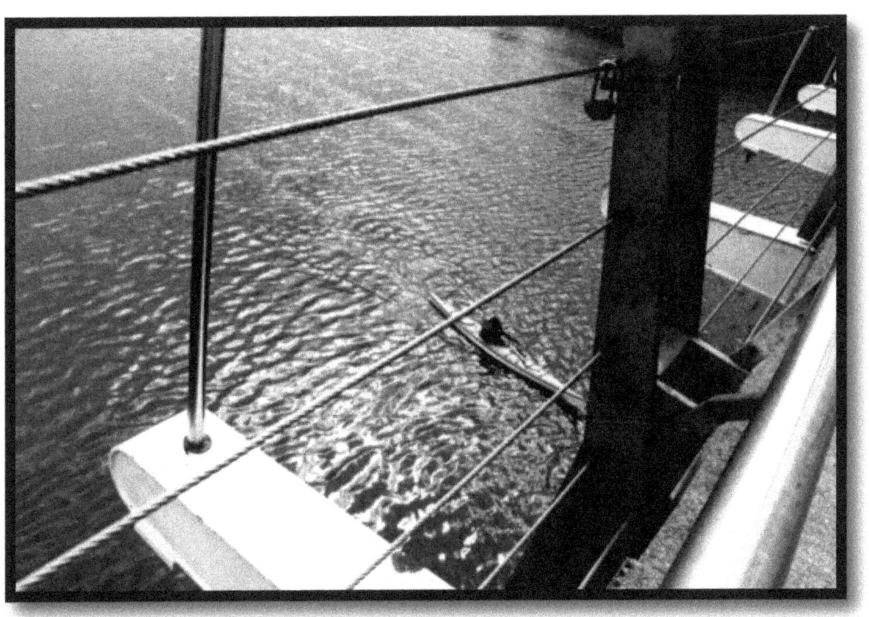

Sue Bracken
Ontario,Sunnyside Kayak

Kaitlyn Langendoen
katylangen07@gmail.com
St. Catharines, Ontario

Port Dalhousie

where the birds, white and black, like a bell,
call on the coming of storms to wash
the heat exhaustion away

where the lake's spray, high and cold, like a sweat,
clings to your face, to say you too can be
weightless, can be made of water

where the light, white and turquoise green, like a sun,
teaches planked piers to be bleached and ships beached
with age and history guided home

where the sails of boards and boats, like a flag,
surrender you to finally stop, watch, and rest
floating willfully lost at sea

where the hills sway back and away, like a buoy,
from the onslaught of Ontario's great lake
and Canadian stay

where the sidewalks of cement and stone, like a drum,
echo the beats, weathered and worn, of bikes and shoes
to lead you back, and back, and back again

where the bakery and cafes narrow and warm, like wellies,
all know you by face, or by name, to say
you have a place

where kilts of clover and twists of pigs, like rum,
blur the bar-tops, tabletops, countertops
into evening meetings and melodies

where the sand in your shoes, like the riverbank,
erodes the skin soft, until easy smiles flow in evening hours
soothing all your jagged worries to songs

the song you know well
the song we sing of Port Dalhousie.

Kate Marshall Flaherty
katiemarshallflaherty@gmail.com
Toronto, Ontario

Standing People

       Dear seedling, future forest figure
       of the standing people,
fires rage red-to-grey right now,
cremating your kin.
Their consuming smoke rises in ashy plumes
all over the continent,

making hazy particulate sunsets,
and we walking people, wake mornings now
to campfire smells in the city and yellow fog.

       Planters planted match sticks
       'til they learned your diversity—mixing now
       all types of trees-to-be, reforesting

as your elders are fast turned to tinder,
and old growth overstory
combusts with brush, out of control—

I wear paper masks again
for the choking smoke,
stay indoors in a wooden home
made of planks from cedar clear-cuts.

I see the grey haze
from a pressure-treated dock,
reading paperback stories,
       utopian times of green past.

Our consumption spreading like wildfire.

Keith Inman
inman@vaxxine.com
Thorold, Ontario

Wind Blown

Along from the bookshop
and new wine boutique
we walk toward the restaurant
with its enclosed porch
and large windows
across from the old
red brick school house
and its
heavy linteled doorways
for Boys
and Girls
carved in stone
looming
over the newly paved drive
and metal sign
for a Lawyer's
– End of Life Service –
ringed by a small garden
of Lilies and Sweet William
glowing under a blue sky
crossed with vapour trails
as we order savoury pie
and café americano
in a room swirling
with accented voices
from around the world
in this
wind-blown heaven

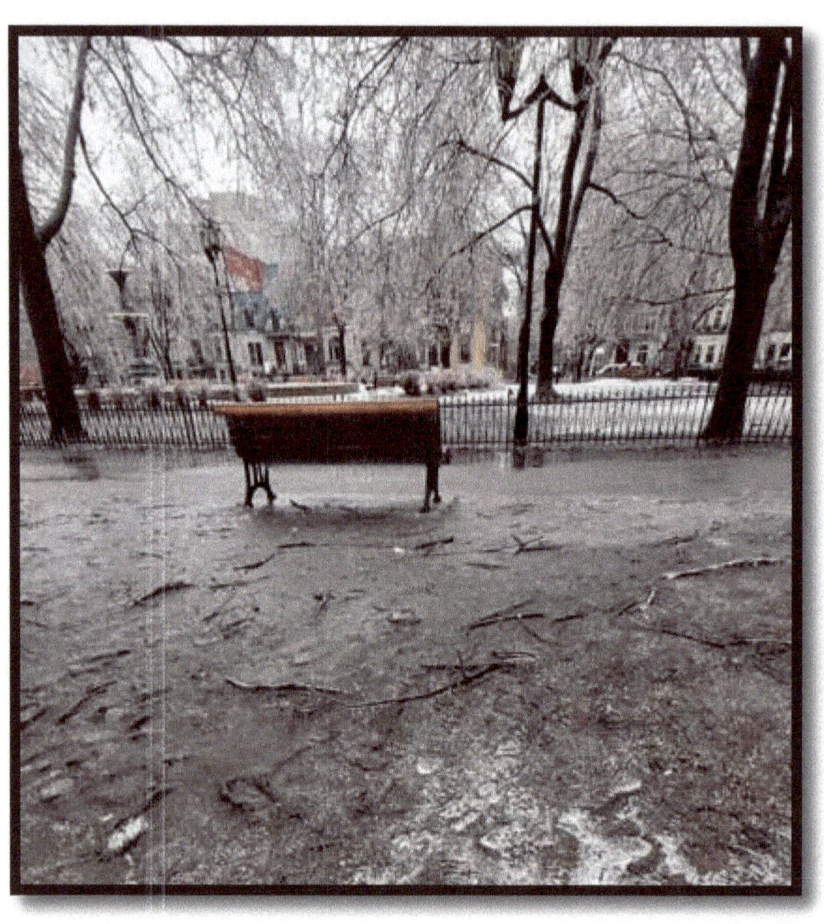

Anna Panunto
Montreal, Quebec

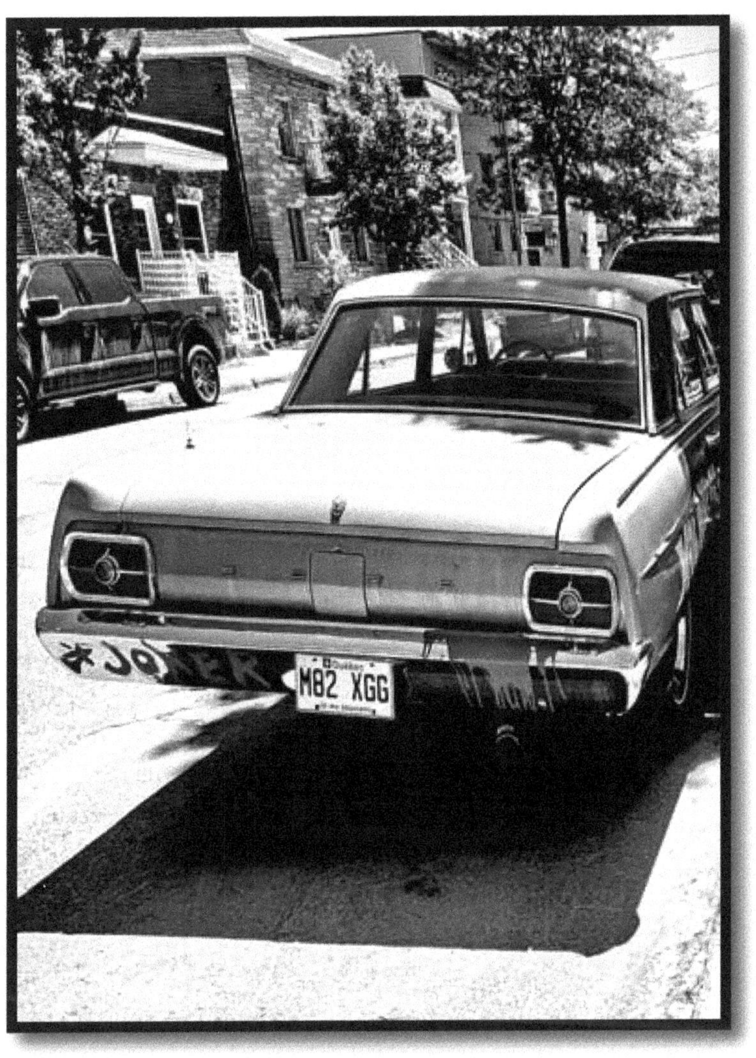

Anna Panunto
Montreal, Quebec

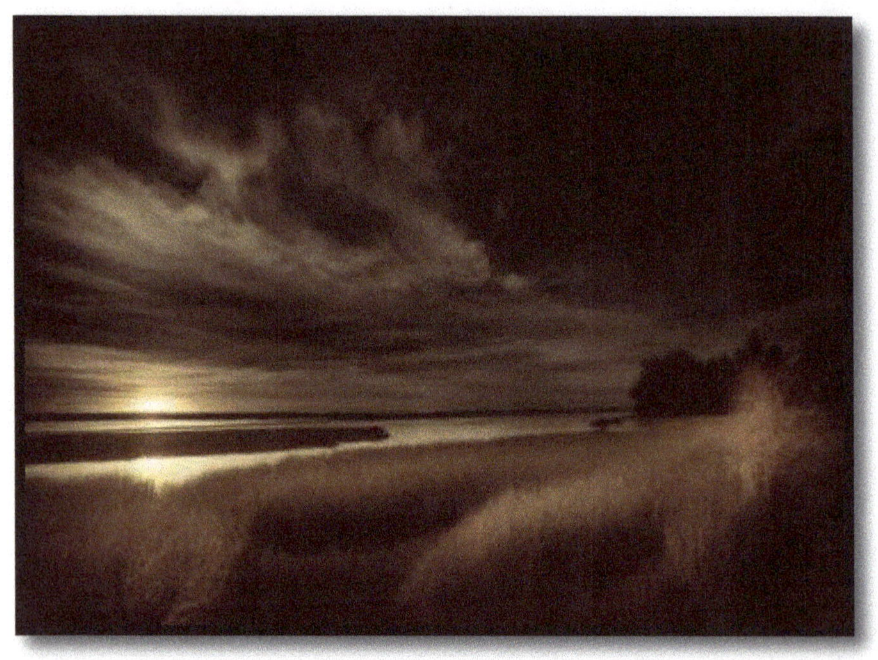

Richard Marvin Tiberius (Tai) Grove
Presqu'ile Provincial Park

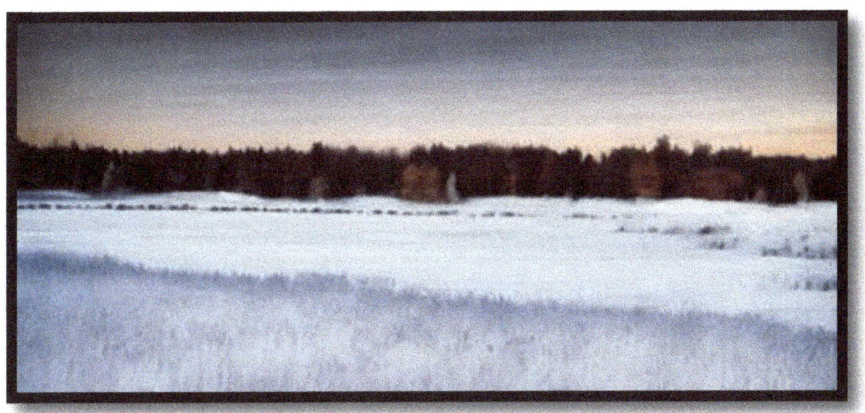

Richard Marvin Tiberius (Tai) Grove
Presqu'ile Provincial Park

Katerina Vaughan Fretwell
kfretwell@cogeco.ca
St. Catharines, Ontario

What Is There

> *I want to stand still*
> *inside the small low room of his life*
> *and recognize him for my sake.* *

Your loving lines extend
the life of a preemie,
cruelly short – a keepsake
for his parents, too stunned
to hold in memory
the tiny limbs, the distilled
presence of their son,
hard to see beyond the bandages,
his mouth craving air, lips pulsing like gills.
I want to stand still,

you wrote, breathing in every line
of this small life, bereft, no fat
to cushion his heroic fight.
Your figure-drawing book *Vision*,
shows how you drew this life,
without preconceptions – rife
with invented terms for torso, leg, head,
so we grasp what's there, not what's expected.
Your gift, a lasting image, outshines the strife
inside the small low room of his life.

If only you could have blessed my mother
with sketches of her five stillbirths
before I arrived, three weeks preemie,
but slowly, slowly thriving.
Vision transports me to your studio
where students intuited the high stakes
to make lines that caress the essence
of a living, breathing life.
You cared, you loved. I offer this brief take
on your kind words: *and recognize him for my sake.*

Good grief! Now your drawings are the keepsake
of your life now deceased!

**Heather Spears, "Undiagnosed," The Word For Sand, (1988), 36*

Lorna Crozier
lornacrozier@shaw.ca
N. Saanich, BC

Chop Sticks

Your childhood awkwardness with a knife and fork is tripled, quadrupled, when it's chopsticks in hand, whether they're compostable, wood thin as the skeletons of model airplanes or tough and artistically rendered, meant to keep and treasure. For your six-month anniversary, your Chinese-Canadian boyfriend who spoke three languages and played Chopin, taught you the lubriciousness of clumps of tea leaves, wet, placed carefully just so, and after, gave you polished, lacquered sticks, each painted with the white, elongated body of a crane. You'd swear the cranes were real, energized, agitating your fingers, making them jump and slip as if they wanted to wade through pools with calico and silver koi instead of the shallow, messy puddle of your bowl.

Your boyfriend, growing bolder, used chopsticks to tease your nipples as if they could be plucked and lifted to his mouth like button mushrooms. Chop sticks as a sex toy was okay, certainly preferable to a fork, though a furred set would have been less pinchy, more inventive on his part, more Dada, one could say.

If he'd come up with that, maybe you'd have fought harder to keep him away from the Danish cyclist who ran into him on Main and who, to make amends, bought him a mango and a bottle of blue gin. In the end, his seemed an effortless goodbye, both of you with no regrets, the snap of wood, the take-out kind, quick as a wishbone's crack and split, though for weeks slivers troubled your fingers just under the skin.

Mike Madill
westerndawn@hotmail.com
Beeton, Ontario

Insomnia

Through my open window comes
mumbled *goodnights*, fading footsteps,
latching doors, even the chatty eucalyptus
trees now settled. It's past twelve, so that
raucous troupe of crying queltehue birds
will soon start their after-hours racket.
Here in Chile, notepad brimming:
menus of Santiago cafes in chalky
Spanish scrawls; loping, saddle-creaking
horseback rides trailing through
thorny espinos; the stone statue of
theVirgin Mary I met in Neruda's library.

The soft clacking of my keyboard,
piecing together something I hope
will wow tomorrow's class –
foothills of bronze and copper grit,
sun-burnt grasses crunching
like wood-chips with every step.

I bend towards the screen, the walls
glowing with indigo obsession.
Shadowed shirts hang from pegs
on the stucco wall, dusty shoes waiting
by the baseboard, my crinkly-clear
water-bottle nearly empty.
Behind me, the bed waits
under a canopy of lazy white netting.
I brush my teeth with slow purpose,
wiggle in ear-plugs, crawl between sheets
only to stare into the dark, wondering
if I'll ever say what I really mean.

Richard-Yves Sitoski
r_sitoski@yahoo.ca
Owen Sound, Ontario

Astronomy with a Microscope

You came from the generation
that put the planets within reach,
mother, so it's natural
that I looked at your finger
when you pointed at the sky.

Like you, mother,
I've misgendered
my share of constellations.
At least I try

though there's a haze between
my lens and the night,
product of a forest fire
a whole world away.

Sorry, I cannot lie.

It's vitreous floaters
in my own damned eye,
and the flames are at my feet,
where I lit them.

Ruth Buckley
r.buckley@bell.net
Kingston, Ontario

Your Man Smell at the Coffee Shop

That heavenly scent wafted from your grave today.
I was in the coffee shop, waiting in line,
when the gentleman in front of me
removed his fur-trimmed winter coat.
My senses stirred, quivered, expectant.
The ghost of your seductive aroma wafted.

Your man smell…so loved, so captivating, so embedded.

I inched closer to the coat, sniffed deeply,
lifted my chin, leaned in, sniffed again
like some forest creature sensing a signal.
My senses sparked, blazed, flamed high.
I sniffed loudly, gulped, greedy for you.
"Oh my God, you smell exactly like my late husband
he died last year you know he was 85 it was
just terrible just awful you know for me and my children
we were married for 65 years you know."

The murmuring in the coffee shop stilled.
The gentleman recoiled, gave me a weak smile.
The cashier, a grey-haired lady, handed me my coffee
and added: *"It's a funny thing about smells, isn't it?"*

Teresa Hall
thallartist@gmail.com
Scarborough, Ontario

The Ice Caps

Evidence of ice drops
melting fast, one by one falling.
Pregnant rivers overflowing,
super storms brewing.
Tall stacks firing, plastic seas
warming, air blackened
by the greed
or was it just ignorance?
Tell that to the generations yet
unborn.
The planet is still rotating
on its axis as the world always has,
keeping that end of the bargain.
Why can't we keep ours?
Wasn't that the price
for giving us the means to
survive?
We in turn take care of the planet.
Haven't we just seen Earth as
a beacon of light across the
universe; a cathedral of life in
the vast barrenness of space?
Why wouldn't we protect
as much as possible?
Many fellow innocents
have succumbed because of us.
But we, the admirers of
sunsets, have the most to
lose of all. Perhaps Earth will
correct the balance.
Perhaps, it will just keep
spinning without us.

Thomas Sinaguglia
Thomassinaguglia@gmail.com
Kingston, Ontario

Before sleep

Before sleep picks apart
The gentle petals of the dark
And lays them down against our eyes

We feel as though something's lost
In daylight, a thought we had
That was not brought to life.

It moves in circles in our minds
Like leaves the wind, inclined
Will spread throughout the solitary evening.

They whisper and hush
Against trees that creak
And long to touch the sky.

Where do they go?
Thoughts like leaves
That tumble and slow,

That drift from branches
And spread apart
Each to cross the Earth alone.

Wendy Jean MacLean
wendyjeanmaclean@gmail.com
Brockville, Ontario

Beloved Bina

My beloved Bina
You were named for understanding
and even your four-year-old wisdom
mimics the way banks and cliffs
hold mighty rivers.

Today I sit on the shore
looking out across the waters.
In my stillness and your current
 (you never stop moving!)
we both find our rest
holding and being held
in this great flow of spirit.

You are still a little girl,
a pebbled collection
of the wonder of your ancestors
and the dreams of your imaginary friends.
Love writes her story in mud
and leaves and sticks in your garden.
Someday your strength will gather
leaders, and their plans
for a new world of peace.
You will give them a voice
with the wisdom you learned
from rivers and rocks
that call you by your secret name.

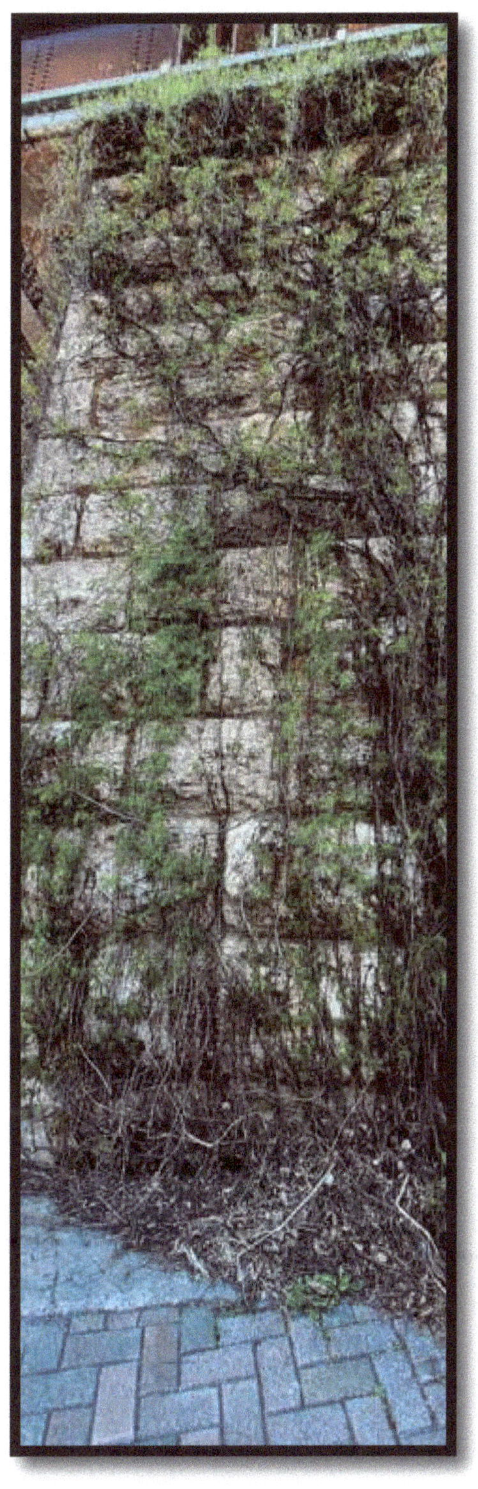

Anna Panunto
Montreal, Quebec

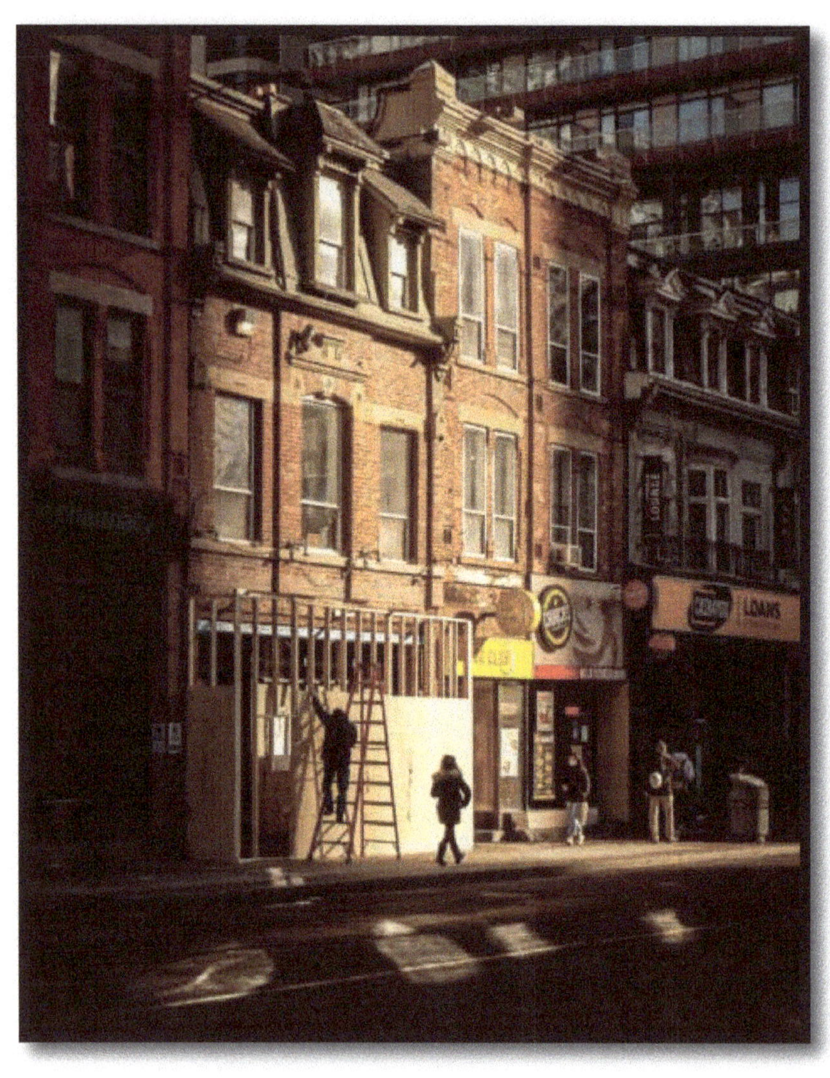

Robin Sutherland

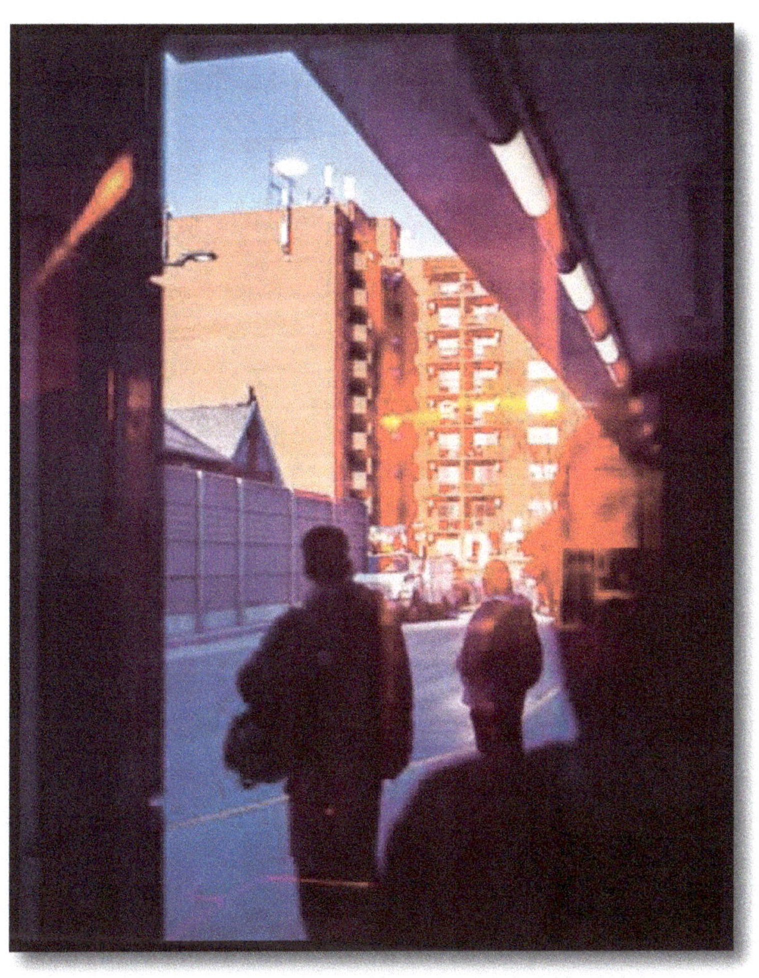

Robin Sutherland

Poem and a Preamble
by John B. Lee

On Christmas Day at dinner my six-year-old grandson posed the question "How do humans make humans?" Shortly before posing that question, he had said that today (meaning Christmas Day) was the day God was born. He and his brother had acquired a pair of bearded dragon lizards only a short while ago. We had been talking briefly about the gender of the lizards, and whether or not they were a male and a female. The larger of the two lizards was named Gizmo, and the lesser of the two was named Larry. Gizmo had mounted Larry at one point, and I wondered if they might produce a clutch of eggs and more lizards. Perhaps that was on his mind. I sat down on Boxing Day morning, and was reading Joy Kogawa's latest book of poems, one I received from my wife Cathy as a Christmas present. As is often the case when I'm reading other poets, I find myself inspired by the spirit of the voice of the poet. The poem I wrote began with my grandson's question, included the lizards, and of course the story of the conception of Jesus, and his. birth. We also spoke briefly about my having visited the church of the Nativity in Bethlehem, and how sad it was this year that all services were cancelled due to the war between Israel and Hamas, though in the poem, I mention the region rather than fall into the honey trap of an opinion on taking one side or the other. To me, warfare is always a failure of the human imagination, and although this particular war may be one on which people have opinions about the justice on either side, it is with every victim, every soldier, every citizen, every human who loses their life by violence with whom I am sympathetic. The phrase "no one is right if everybody's wrong," comes to mind. And the words from the song "I'm just a poor boy whose intentions are good, oh Lord, oh Lord, don't let me be misunderstood," also come to mind. Here's the poem.

How Do Humans Make Humans

seated at the festive table
on Christmas day
my six-year-old grandson
inquires of me
"Grandpa, how do humans
make humans?"

he had been talking
about this being
the day God was born

not God, I said
the son of God
conceived of Mary by the Holy Spirit
brought forth of an angel
the baby Emanuel
born in a manger in Bethlehem

meanwhile
the bearded dragons
in the lizard aquarium
seem to be coupling
as we adults consider
how to answer the little boy's question

he who is so innocent of the knowledge
of the cloacal kiss
I talk of trees
and of the pollinating drones
of male and female
in every species of mammal
of dogs and horses
of men and women
of fathers and mothers
with his older brother smirking nearby
to think of a question
each generation asks of another
the one we all understand, eventually

as this year in Bethlehem
the silence deafens all believers
because of the war
with the great unmaking of humans
in Israel, the Gaza strip

as the angel covers the virgin
and so the story goes …

and everywhere lovers
like seed kites
explode on the wind
like the grass that catches the snow

Indigenous Canada
∆ⁱⁱᴘ / IHKE / MAKING/ART

∆ⁱⁱᴘ is the phonetic spelling of "IHKE" in the Indigenous language.
IHKE" is the root word of "Make" in the Indigenous language.

Indigenous Curator
Debora Puricelli

Welcome to the Indigenous Making/Art section of Devour: Art & Lit Canada. My name is débora Uᐟᵇ◁ Puricelli >ᵇ∆⁻▽ᵉᵉ∆. My prayers friend from early adulthood, who also shares Indigenous heritage, reminded me that I didn't add a tribe and/or clan and/or Nations as part of my introduction in the previous issue so here I will include a note to explain and clarify further to this beautiful reminder. I am part of a clan from the Kennedy heritage and I am part of a tribe from the Zemma heritage and I am part Kiwi from the New Zealand part of the Lowe side and finally I am part First Nations from the Turtle Island part from the North Shore of Quebec Dubé. I feel like the Four directions are represented in this story of heritage and culture and soul where my love for Making/Art comes from. I still believe that spelling out heritage is always a good place to stay and live in. Thanks again for this prayers friend from Six Nations, my reminder, who I called Elder, even though in age, she is younger than I am, positive that Truth and talents and trust of this person has helped me to overcome great obstacles in my life. This said I would like to introduce, Robin Sutherland, the Indigenous Artist Photographer for this issue of Devour.

Robin and I met, I believe, in 1996 back when I was surviving life as a bicycle messenger. I had just changed companys and I knew some of the folks from his company and somehow we ended up speaking while ending my break. Robin and I recently bumped into each other at Pape subway station and we chatted, like we once did, about his recent dive into Photography. The photograph he showed me was of two trains at a subway station with a visual fragment of people on the other side through the reflective surface of two trails passing. Much like the stories of our passing paths as couriers. Life is cyclical by Nature.

Nature reviews our place as part of the Making/Art process. On my walk to figure out how to say what I need to say nature reminds me of autonomy and how nature doesn't discriminate against anyone and/or anything. Nature's acceptance of every identity is absolute and/or whole. Nature is not labeling and or discriminating but accepting of all. As an example, when I am walking and I see litter in Nature, I am still labeling that stuff/litter as litter. Nature is not doing that. Nature teaches us these important reminders/lessons each and every day for all. Nature as acceptance and Making/Art as process and/or conversations about these lessons from Nature. Wind as a sculptor weaving through us, the people of the Land of the place of Nature. Peace, stay safe and kind.

Biographical Note for Debora Puricelli

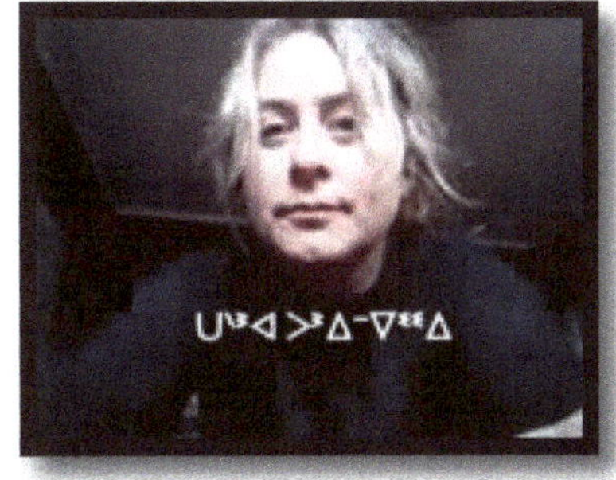

débora ᑎᐧᔓᐊ puricelli ᕉᐟᐃᐨᐁᔰᐃ graduated from the Indigenous Visual Culture Program at OCADU in 2018. She received the Bronze award for Highest marks in Liberal Arts and Sciences as well as the award for Highest achievement in the INVC (Indigenous Visual Culture Program). She was also given the title of "Knowledge Keeper" or "Knowledge Holder" by the Ojibwe/Cree Elders, Edna and Connor.

Peace Kwe.

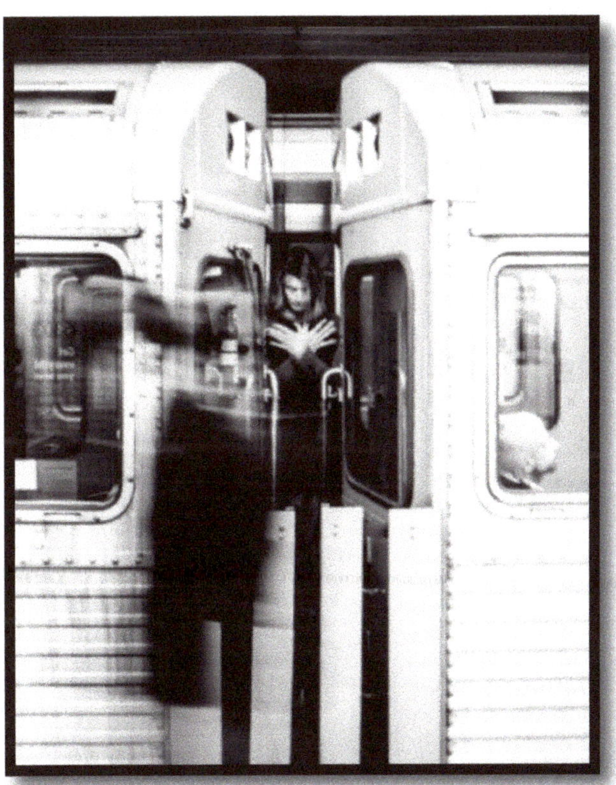

Robin Sutherland

Robin Sutherland, Indigenous Photographer

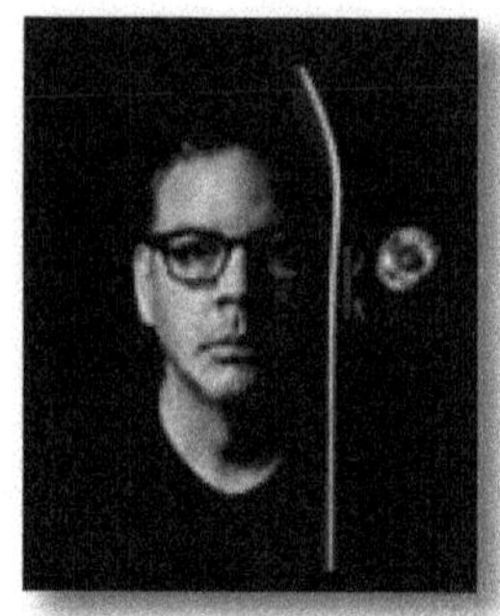

Robin Sutherland

At the beginning of Covid-19, I lost vision in my left-eye. I sank into an overwhelming sadness. Then around 2022, I started walking for my health. I took my camera on these walks. At some point I realized that having vision in only one eye, to a degree, made me see as though I were looking at a two dimensional world or at a photograph. Photographers close one eye to see a possible photo better; I do this on a permanent basis. This new vision, combined with the fact that I am native in a largely nonnative city, makes me see the world as though I am an alien. I belong but don't belong. I see but I see differently.

I am a Cree and Ojibway visual storyteller from Rama Ontario, now based in Toronto. I am a self-taught photographer who has been making images for over twenty years. I make only the barest edits to images and choose to capture the world from a different perspective.

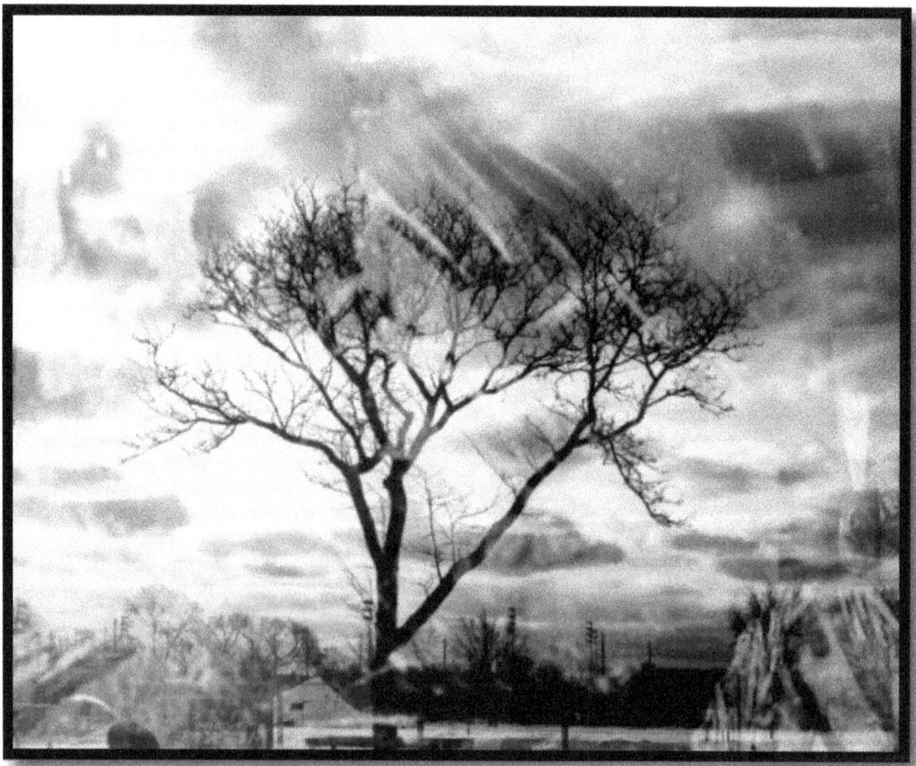

Robin Sutherland

When asked about my photographs, Bita Sazegara, a contemporary photographer remarked, "when I'm looking at them, they give me familiar and strange feeling at the same time … they are the locations we see every day, but somehow, … they are from [an] alternate universe, [a] parallel universe. They kind of seem they are from [a] dream world."

Link to my work.
Instagram: @Robin.suth

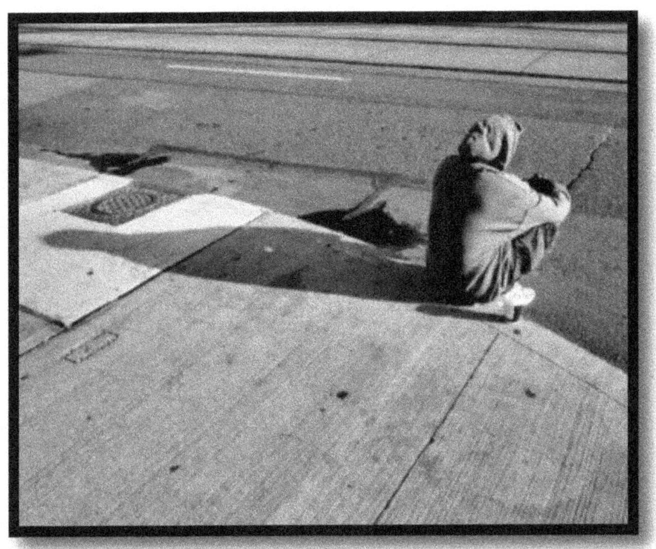

Robin Sutherland

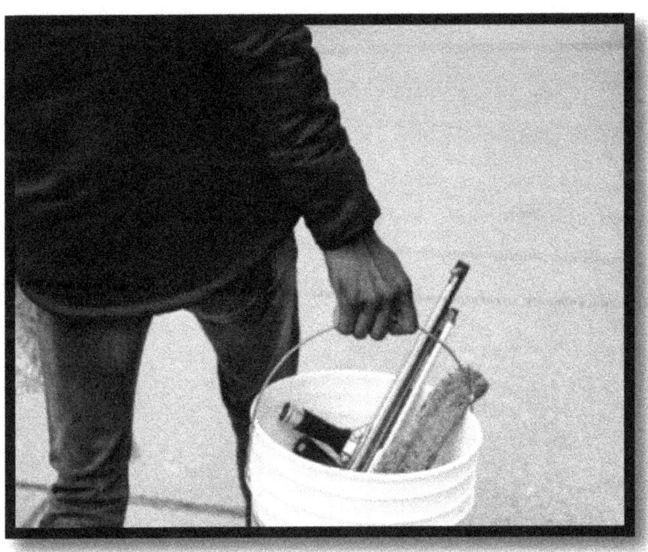

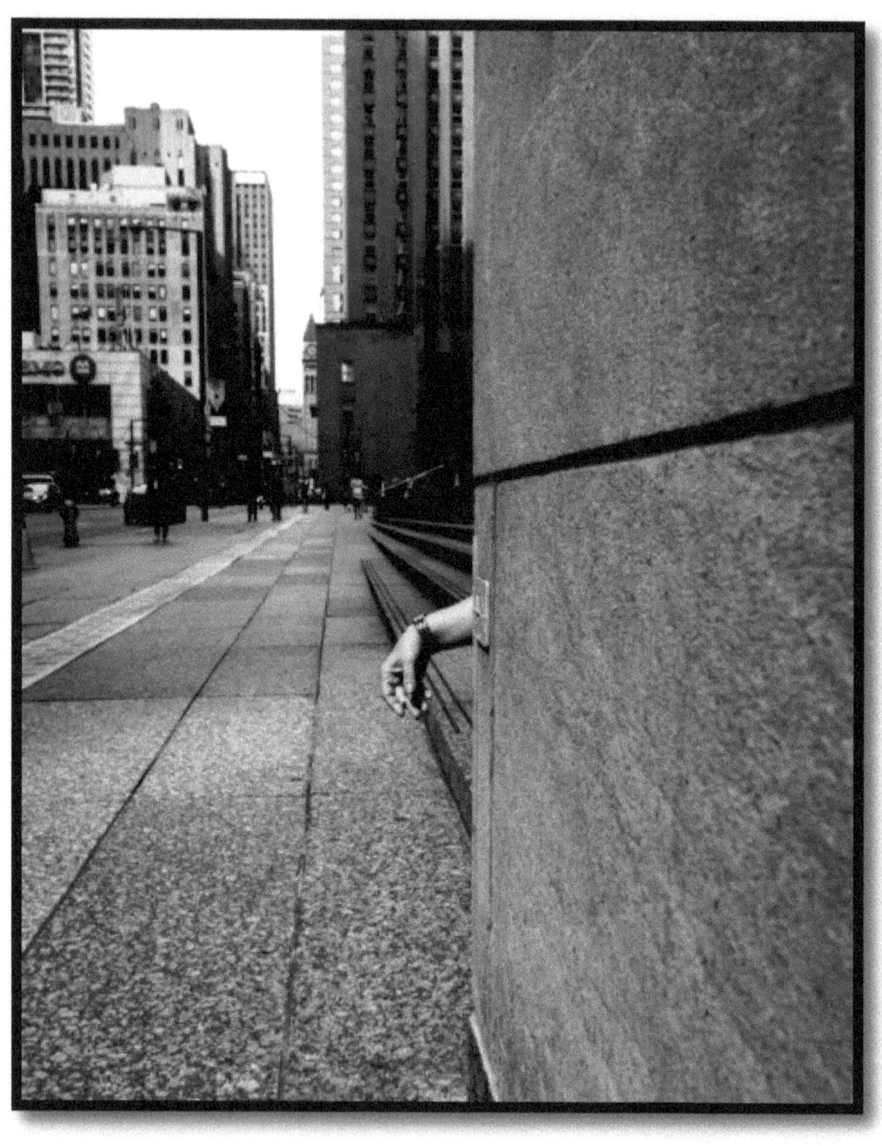

Robin Sutherland

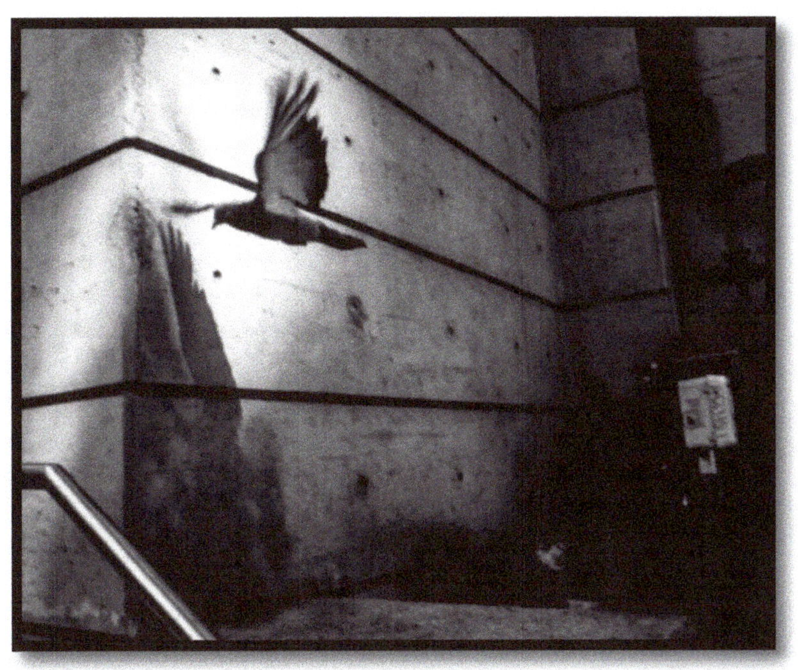

Robin Sutherland

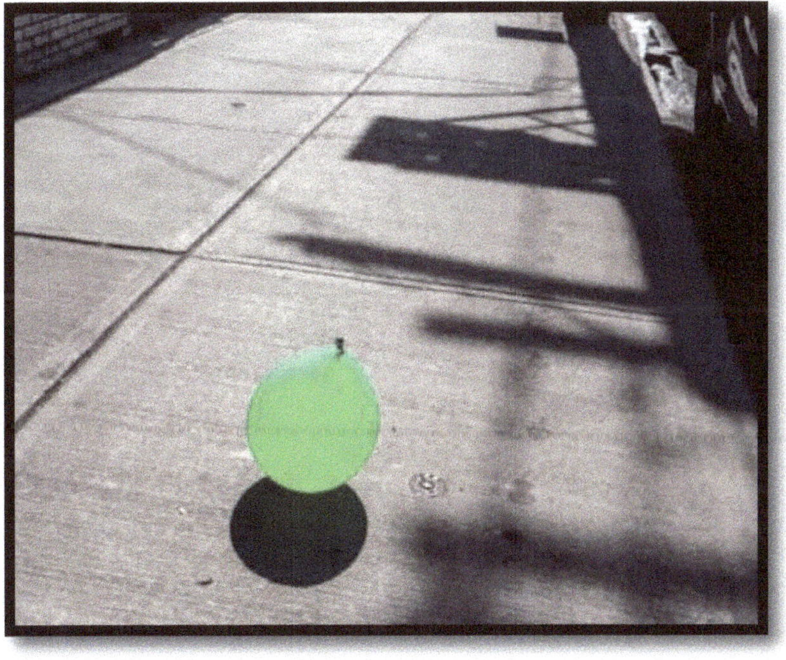

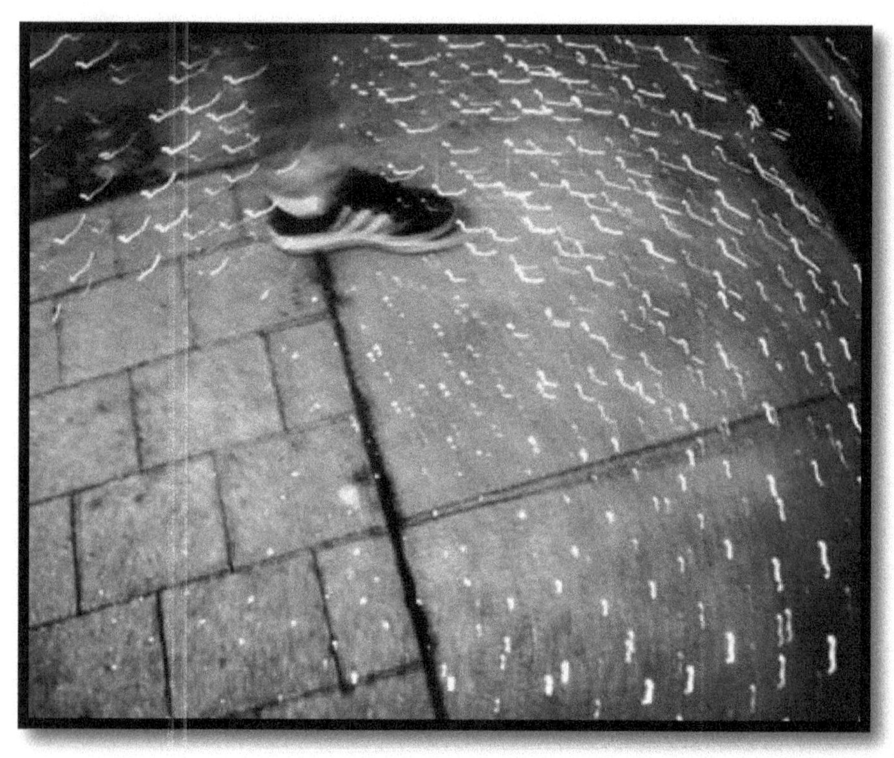

Robin Sutherland

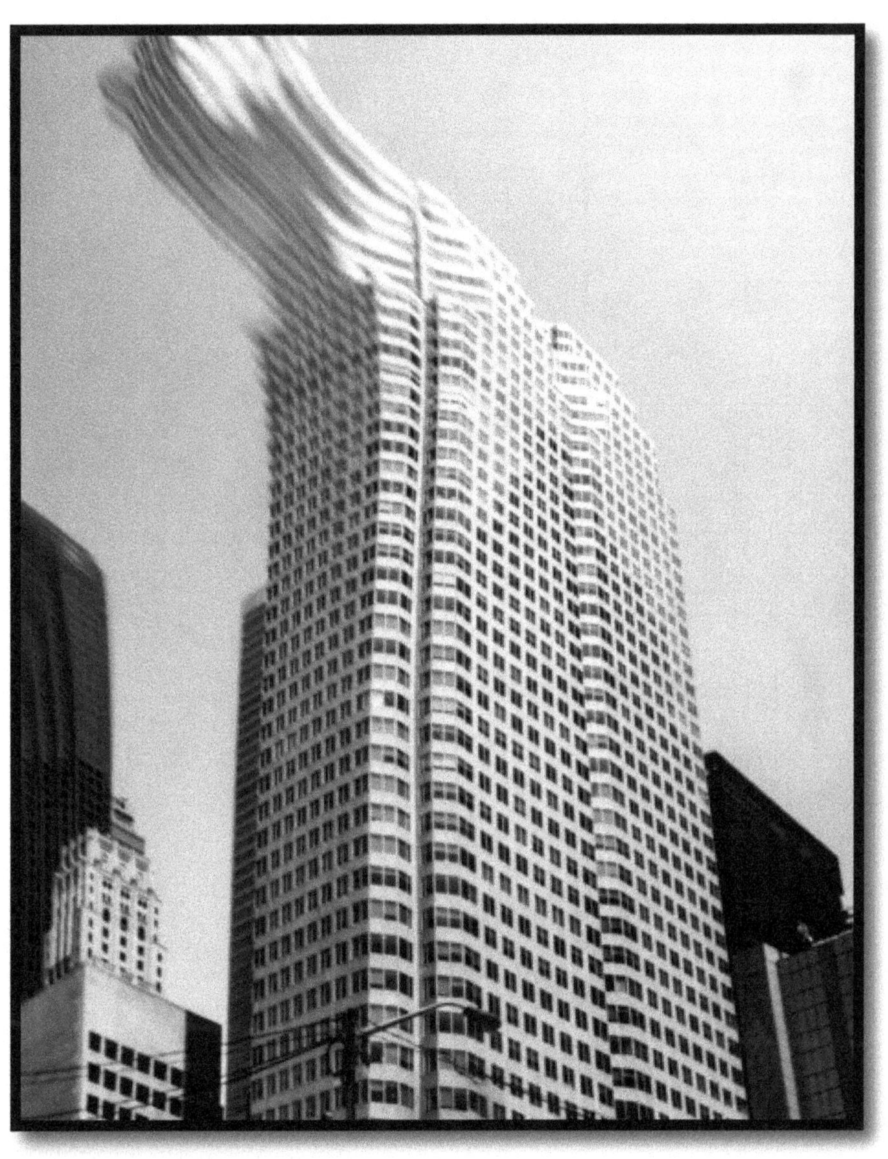

Robin Sutherland

Canada in Prose

Prose Curator – Brian Moore

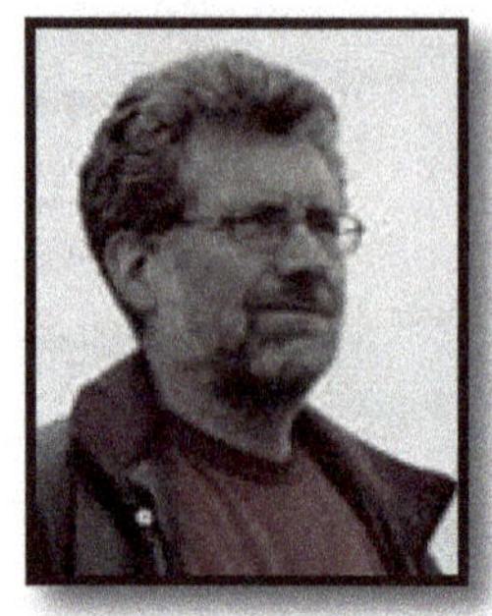

Dear fellow readers. This is just a quick note to say thank you to Brian Moore for stepping up as the Prose Curator for this new section. Click on some of the links below to find his work. We look forward to reading his picks. *Richard M. Grove / Tai - Publisher.*

Bio note for Brian Moore – December 2023

Brian Moore lives in Toronto where he worked as a project manager in the financial services industry. He has been writing prose for 6 years and has had over a dozen stories published internationally in periodicals such as Blank Spaces, The Barren, October Hill, and Event.

He feels honoured to serve as Prose Curator for Devour: Art & Lit Canada and is looking forward to showcasing some of the best in new Canadian prose.

You can find some of Brian's recent work at:

– **"Cherry Red Witch,"** Event Magazine, v51, #1 –
https://www.eventmagazine.ca/product/event-511-digital/
– **"Swimming with Girls,"** October Hill, Spring 2022 –
https://drive.google.com/file/d/1eIHX434IneLwRd2WjEyjsn3xSRTn3BGg/view?pli=1
– **"The White Boats,"** Valparaiso Fiction Review, V10, #1 –
https://scholar.valpo.edu/vfr/vol10/iss1/7/
– **"A Store for Men,"** The Blotter, August 2020 – pp. 9 - 14
http://www.blotterrag.com/pdfs/2020-08.pdf
– **"Before You Leap,"** Gordon Square Review, #6 –
http://www.gordonsquarereview.org/brian-moore.html

Run Over Dog

by Brian Moore

Hamid saw his daughter and her boyfriend in the parking lot at the high school, loitering near the tennis courts. Both of them wore knapsacks and unzipped hoodies and running shoes with laces spilling loose on the asphalt. He should not have seen them. He had no business being there. It was a work day and he should have been in the store, making money. But he had to know. He sat in his car, barely twenty feet away, the heater huffing out of the dash and his breath fogging the window. Their absorption in each other was so complete that he was invisible. She would not have understood his curiosity and his worry, his dread that something was going to happen that could not be taken back. She would have hated him for his selfishness.

Laleh was only fourteen, still in braces, her body shot up into adolescence overnight, into dangling arms and legs and a long pale face. She was dedicated to her studies, a serious, book-bound girl, who scribbled essays on Macbeth late into the evenings under the halo of a desk lamp in her room, who would have worked all night if Hamid didn't order her to sleep. Hamid had not expected her to start dating so soon. Don't interrogate her, his sister warned him over the phone from Tehran. Don't make a mess of things.

The school had a bad reputation for drugs and there were rumours of knives in lockers, used condoms in the bathrooms. It was hopeless to ask Laleh for information. A switch had flipped. She had gone from babbling everything about school to a shroud of secrecy and silence. He had only found out about the boy by accident, when she left her phone unlocked on the kitchen counter and he saw the text. *Meet you at Tim's. I got u bae. Don't be late. Luv 4ever.*

They were apart from the other teenagers. Laleh had waves of thick, black hair, like her mother, cinched into a single ponytail by a quiet, mauve ribbon. She had begun plucking her eyebrows but did not wear makeup, did not need to. Her eyes never left the boy. He said something, blank-faced, and she tilted her chin up, and squeezed his shoulder. He must have been at least a foot taller than her. She leaned into him, lifted up on her toes, ready to be kissed. They had an obscene ease with each other's bodies, as if they had memorized all the caresses and crevices and expressions months ago.

His hand covered her hand. Her skin was white and transparent against his. His hand was black.

Hamid drove home instead of returning to the store. His floor manager could lock up. Hamid opened the door and the dog, Hugo, leapt up, leaving dusty paw prints on Hamid's coat. Hugo was a tall, lean Labrador with a tail like a whip that banged against Hamid's calves, as if the dog spent the whole day in the foyer, impatient for joy and attention. Hamid clipped the leash to Hugo's collar, and let the dog run the length of it out toward the sidewalk, yanking on his arm. It was almost four o'clock. He didn't want to be in the house when Laleh came home. He needed to think.

Hamid considered himself a well-educated man. Before the store he had completed degrees in mechanical engineering and business administration. He had traveled across Europe and the United States, spoke three languages, and had friends who were Chinese and Jewish and Indian. Moderation came easily to him. People respected him. Even the surly, never-satisfied customers listened when he used his Calm Voice, the one that implied fairness, that made them feel embarrassed that they had been upset. So why had he felt a sudden seizing in his gut, as if he had been punched, when he saw that boy's arm around his daughter? Why were the words *that* boy?

He had only Laleh. His wife, Maya, died while Laleh was still a toddler. She had been visiting friends, driving home, when a semi crossed into her lane and t-boned the Honda with so much force that the compact rolled four times before coming to a rest in the median. Her head broke against the roof like an egg dropped on a marble floor. She never woke.

The rest of their family lived overseas, except for a scattering of distant cousins in Toronto. None of them were Laleh's age. Forays into heritage school to learn Farsi had faltered and failed after three months. It was so hard to ground her in Persian culture when it was just the two of them, the future flooding over them day and night. He accepted, without repentance, that he was an over-protective father. He was afraid of losing her.

It was not racism. He was sure.

Hugo dragged Hamid to the park, yanking side to side, investigating. Hamid unclipped the leash and Hugo trotted to the jungle gym, lifted his hind leg and urinated on the tether ball pole. He sniffed the sand around the bottom of the slide. A centimeter of snow laced the ground.

Hugo was his sister's idea. She said Laleh needed something else in the house, to fill it up, to make them feel like a full, overcrowded family, with noises and chaos and messes. A child needs something of her own to take care of. Laleh named him after a cartoon she saw on television.

Hamid had dated for years before he met Maya. When they met, he was almost thirty, grooved into routine, with a comfortable job and an apartment in Toronto. She burst into his life at a farewell party for a friend, like a cat pouncing on a mouse. She was not his type at all: loud, aggressive, stubborn. She had shallow cheekbones and a wide, thin mouth that was moving from the time she woke until she slept. He could not make her keep still. His need to anticipate every detail drove her to distraction. She broke and scattered and threw her laughter like a pennant into the air while he watched, sorting and organizing, cleaning up the corners, making his world small enough to control. The night they first slept together she came into his bedroom and said, *What is this?* What do you mean, he asked. *This! You still lay your clothes out on the bed for morning? What, are you nine?* She tossed them to the floor. Even though he was angry he loved her for it.

He wished he knew the boy's name. After Maya died he'd made a clean break, taken Laleh north to a small town, and opened the carpet store with his savings. One of the few risks he had ever taken and a bad one. A tearing out of roots. They were surrounded by Irish and Scots, Germans and Dutch. Probably only a half-dozen African-Canadian families in the whole place. If he had a surname for the boy, he could ask around. He would know what to expect.

He shivered. It was getting late and the air had a wet feeling of early snow. The park was empty. Where was Hugo?

He whistled and called.

He heard a car horn, a thump, and an engine revving and disappearing east. A row of cedars blocked his view of the street that bordered the park. He began running.

Something lay in the middle of the road.

From a distance he saw a shadow, like a crumpled bag blown off the back of a truck. Hamid pounded up in his leather boots, his tie and jacket flapping, the leash forgotten in his fist. Hugo lay stretched on his side, legs splayed wide, tongue rolled out like a pink ribbon. Hamid knelt and a puddle soaked through the knees of his pants.

There were no skid marks. Whoever hit him had never stopped.

Hugo blinked slowly. A breeze ruffled his blond coat. His flank rose and sank in quick, desperate spasms. A pool of blood like jelly circled his belly.

Hamid didn't know what to do.

He was five blocks from the house. He patted his pockets for his phone, then remembered he had left it on the table in the foyer to charge. The street was empty, a cul-de-sac. Another car might not pass for an hour.

He gently lifted Hugo's head into his lap. When he stroked the dog's ribs it groaned, coughed, and the tail swept the slush.

He would have to carry him back to the house. All seventy pounds. He slid his arm under Hugo's shoulder but Hugo yelped immediately, snapping his teeth. Hamid felt the broken bone stabbing against the fur and sat back on his heels again.

He brushed the dog's ears. Hamid's nose began to run and he wiped at it with his sleeve. For several minutes there was nothing but the cold and the limbs of the trees creaking, rubbing against the wind. It was late November. A crisp, resolute sky; the edge of winter.

Hugo seemed to stop breathing but then his head rolled up towards Hamid, as if asking him a great, longing question, *why, why this*, followed by a deep gasp that shook him end to end, his whole body one final quest for air. The jaws froze. Grey fluid oozed from the anus.

Hamid sank to the road, to his elbows. The breeze dampened, carried off the Lake, and seeped through his jacket. His cheeks began to burn as the temperature dropped. All around him were comfortable, suburban houses, with curtains drawn and, further away, the sounds of distant traffic and sirens, urban conversation, the world going onward. He was surprised to find tears on his cheeks, on his lips. The sun leaked down from the sky, uninvolved.

A pickup, spattered with mud, turned onto the street, and rolled towards him on fat, deep-treaded tires. The truck slowed and stopped. A woman rolled down the window.

"Yours?"

Hamid nodded.

"Jeez, that's a shame," she said. "You okay?"

"Yes."

"Sonsobitches. The way some people drive. That's a beautiful-lookin' dog." She climbed down from the truck. She might have been the same age as Hamid.

"Poor fella," she said. She squatted and rested her hand on Hugo's side. "You didn't deserve that, didya darlin?"

"Do you have a phone?" Hamid asked.

"No. I don't carry those things. Where do you live?"

He waved vaguely.

"I'll give you a lift." He couldn't think of a good reason to say no. He pushed his arms under Hugo, lifted him, and lay his body in the bed of the pickup. He got into the cab and the woman did a U-turn. Her name was Caitlyn.

When they reached the house Laleh was still not home. Out with her boyfriend, he supposed, enjoying herself. He dug a cardboard box out of the garage, made a bed of old blankets and put Hugo inside. He covered the box and pushed it into the utility shed. He had to make sure Laleh didn't see the body until he had told her. He did not know how he could tell her. It was his fault, letting Hugo run free of the leash.

"Would you like to come in?" he asked.

"No, I don't want to bother you."

"It's no bother. Please."

He unlocked the door and led her inside.

"I hope tea is okay. We're not coffee-drinkers."

"Sure." She glanced around at the pictures of his family on the walls, the ornate rug in the living room, the Farsi newspaper on the table. "Where you from?"

"We're from Toronto. Yonge and Finch."

"I mean originally. You're not from here."

When would Hamid ever be from *here*? Twenty years? Thirty?

"I emigrated from Iran." He added, trying not to sound insulting: "In the Middle East."

She nodded and her mouth formed an "Oh", as if she had guessed right.

He set a delicate cream pitcher and sugar bowl on the table. She finally removed her coat, revealing two more sweaters underneath. He carried the tea to her. Maya had bought the tea service in Iran, before she died.

Caitlyn raised the cup, fingers all the way around it as if it were a bowl, and said, "I'm sorry about your dog. They become just like one of the family, don't they? There's no replacing them."

"I don't know what I'm going to tell my daughter. We've had Hugo since he was a pup."

Caitlyn loved dogs, often more than people, who were always searching for ways to let you down. She said she lived just outside of town. She waitressed at a restaurant up on the hill but she and the owner's wife did not get along. Before that Caitlyn did books for Underwood Electrical but it folded, like most of the plants around here.

She asked: "Are you married?"

He pointed to Maya's picture on the mantle in the living room. He had told the story of the accident so many times that it was polished with wear, like a small, smooth stone you pick up on a beach. He should have traveled with Maya that day. He had told her he was too busy at work. The guilt took up a narrow space in his chest, black and lumpish. He touched it late at night when he could not sleep, reminding himself, to see if it still hurt, if it still bled.

Caitlyn understood. She hadn't meant to intrude. She had been married herself but things soured and her husband had gone west to find work. Now, she spent a lot of time reading and taking walks. She had stopped watching television. It was all junk anyway.

"I don't like change," she said.

He nodded. It was good to know that something as simple as the love of an animal could be shared across cultures and religions and continents. He saw that in the way Caitlyn had stroked Hugo's back.

He imagined Laleh and her boyfriend walking hand in hand from school, wrapped inside themselves, and he felt terribly alone.

Caitlyn stretched forward, wiggling the cold out of her toes, wool socks on her feet.

"You know what your girl would like?"

"What?"

"A horse. All girls love horses."

She explained that she rented a house and a small barn on a five-acre lot and the owner, a lawyer, wintered in Miami this time of year. Part of the deal was that he gave her a break on the rent if she took care of a mare that stabled in the barn. The mare was a quarter horse, a kind of pet, with a chestnut coat and a white blaze down the forehead.

"You could bring your girl out any time. I won't mind. It's good for a horse to stay used to people or they start getting nervous. There's a saddle and a tack room. I could harness the mare and your daughter could ride her around, nice and slow, inside the corral."

"She would like that," Hamid said. "That's very generous."

She stood and he followed her to the door. She wrote her name and number on a pad on the foyer table. If there was anything he needed, just call her. Let her know ahead and she would harness the mare and brew some tea for both of them.

She said she appreciated that he wasn't like some people.

"What do you mean?"

"Some people come here and they expect the rest of us to accommodate them. I think that's just rude, don't you? You're not like that at all."

He walked her out to her truck. She waved and smiled as she backed out and turned into the street. He noticed for the first time that there was a black sticker on the rear bumper. In white letters the sticker read: *Welcome to Canada. Fit In or Fuck Off.*

While he watched, the pickup passed Laleh on the sidewalk, a block away. His daughter swished her toes through a carpeting of dead leaves, head down. Her face brimmed with astonishing secrets. She was young and love was a new thing.

Out loud, he said: *Maya.* The name expanded, grew into white breath in the air, rose like incense.

Maya, I am still in love with you.

"Run Over Dog." was originally published in an online magazine called "Orson's Review", Apr 14, 2020, which is no longer online.

Feature Prose Writer:
Lois Hibbert

Intro by Brian Moore

I first met Lois Hibbert a few years ago in a writers' group in North York. She was working on her first novel, a book about a young woman struggling to overcome the trauma of sexual assault by a person of trust. Lois read the novel to us, a chapter at a time, over several months, until we grew to know and care about the characters as if they were real people sitting at the table with us. Lois brought empathy, courage, and honesty with every draft. She is a woman of strong values and self-deprecating humour, always ready with a kind word and a keen eye for improvements that strengthened the writing of other members in the group.

In the piece I asked Lois to submit for this issue, she reflects on her mother and their relationship—a personal history of hardships, joys, and family. Her mother's journey is a life well-lived, before the comforts of technologies that most of us have forgotten we are so reliant upon. Parents have passed, a husband has come and gone, children were raised, grandchildren adored, griefs endured.

There may come a time, for those fortunate enough to have longevity, when they are "so tired." They have exhausted all the milestones, wrung out all the big moments of love and birth and friendship. My own father taught me to be grateful for the smallest moments of each day: a joke, a sunrise, laughter, someone to hold your hand. In the time that you have, do what is needed. Make peace with your mistakes and the blows everyone suffers. Be prepared to release life. Then, maybe, at the end of a long life, we'll be ready for it to release us.

Lois Hibbert is a long-time Toronto, Ontario resident who finds that "What if?" questions lead her in unexpected directions for short stories and flash fiction. She also enjoys short creative non-fiction writing to record events and explore memories.

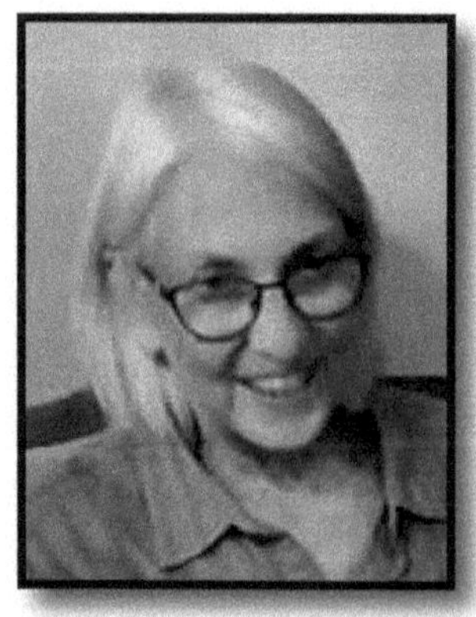

Lois Hibbert

So Tired

by Lois Hibbert

I wonder how I got so old so fast.

> *I imagine my mother asking this as she neared her 99th birthday as the world around her blurred and became quieter. Did her memories of long ago yesterdays inch into today?*

Yesterday I was riding in a buggy with my dad, horsehair blanket tucked around me, while he delivered mail to the farmers around our little town, learning the commands for the horses to turn or stop or go—gee, haw, whoa, giddy-up. Today, I give up writing, my hand unsteady on the page, and I wait for letters that mostly don't come.

> *Mom rarely talked about her childhood but we know, from a memories project that my daughters did with her and Dad, that he gave up his job as a sailor when he got married, thinking life on the water wasn't good for a family man. And we all learned one of her very vivid childhood memories from a game where you had to flip over cards and try to remember where the matching card was. One of the pairs was of a snake— a cartoon one, but it was enough. If anyone turned it over, she remembered precisely where that card was and if she turned over the matching card even much later, she'd scream and unerringly go back to the first one. All dated back to a Massassauga rattler getting into their house when she was about seven. That'd do it.*

Yesterday I learned to read and discovered that words on a page could take me so much farther than any journey in a buggy or car or train or airplane. Today, even large print blurs and wobbles and I travel those distances only in my memory.

> *One of those travels took her to Rosedale, a wealthy neighbourhood in Toronto, after living through the Great Depression as a teenager and leaving school after Grade 8. Why did I never ask why she had to leave school? Were there fewer teachers in her small village on the Bruce Peninsula? Where would education have taken her? Probably not to a small rural community as a farmer's wife.*

Yesterday my world expanded as I left a small village and home where I knew everyone and moved to a big city where I knew no one at first, cleaning houses for rich people. I dreamed of becoming a nurse but became a Nurse's Aide instead, the best I could do with Grade 8. Today, Nurse's Aides get me to the dining room, bathe me, and help me to the bathroom and into and out of bed.

Mom occasionally spoke of enjoying her time in Toronto, coming to know and love a step-sister after Mom's widowed father married Vi's widowed mother. But Dad was persistent after he met her in church when she was posted for experience as a nurse's aide in his rural community, making the 80-mile trek to Toronto in a Model A Ford once a month to court her. What if she had never been posted to that small town? What would her life have looked like as a city woman?

Yesterday I married a good man, an honest man who had dreams of becoming a veterinarian but, like me with only a grade school education, abandoned that dream and took over the family farm, in the same community with many relatives.

I cannot imagine her adjustment to the reality of life as a farmer's wife. Early morning breakfast, dinner at noon, supper at 6:00, feeding crews during seeding and harvesting, growing enough vegetables for the winter months, canning, preserving, and, of course, children, four in six years and a fifth four years later. Trying to accept Dad's work ethic—she said she could never understand why Dad worked even in foul weather when other farmers stayed inside. If there wasn't an obvious job, Dad would find something—chopping wood, fixing an implement, working in the barn.

She hinted occasionally at an uneasy relationship with Dad's sisters. I remember the one who lived closest as being very strong-willed, almost the opposite of Mom's much more reserved personality. And the sisters in Dad's family all went through high school—did they look down on her, because she was less educated, not recognizing the difference between education and intelligence? Or because she moved from the city, did they maybe not see her as a true farmer's wife? She got along very well with two sisters-in-law, married to Dad's brothers who farmed nearby. Maybe they commiserated together.

Did she feel cut off from her own family, surrounded as she was by many of Dad's relatives in the community? She didn't talk often about her siblings other than that there had been a severely disabled institutionalized older sister and a younger brother who died of diphtheria. It always seemed like a happy event when one of her sisters or brothers and families visited or we all piled into the car to visit them. But of her younger brother Howard, emotionally and in age closest to her, all we have is a photograph of a handsome young man in army uniform before being shipped overseas to fight.

My brother Howard didn't come home from the war, dying at 21 in the liberation of Belgium, the news arriving in the afternoon as I was preparing a meal for a harvest crew of eight. I put their food on the table as I fought tears and cared for a three-year-old and an infant, praying that they would never have to go to war. Today, a solemn newscaster tells me that a young woman has died fighting for peace in a far off country in a war that has dragged on for decades and that will have only losers.

My heart aches for her when I remember Dad telling us that she was even quieter than usual as she fed that harvest crew and didn't tell him about Howard until the evening. Now we can bookend that earlier photo with one my youngest daughter took when she placed flowers at Howard's grave in a meticulously maintained cemetery in Belgium that she visited in 2013. Mom was moved to tears by the photo; I hope it was a comfort to her that Howard was remembered and honoured with so many others.

Her strength awes me. And when I look at the date, I believe she may have already been pregnant with the third baby—she may not have even known it then.

Yesterday I was toilet training my kids, praying for relief from constant caring and the drudgery of soaking, rinsing, and washing cloth diapers that turned grey after so much use. Today I use adult protection against "leaks" and hope an aide or nurse will come before the leaks leak.

One of my earliest memories may relate to her hoping for a rare break from constant child care. A quiet afternoon in our screened-in front porch, lying at the opposite end to Mom on a big old brown overstuffed sofa. None of my siblings were around, perhaps at school, and I think now, having experienced the exhaustion of caring for children myself, that Mom was probably hoping I would go to sleep. I remember feeling complete security, just Mommy and me, and then I presumably cooperated and nodded off in the drowsy heat.

Did she regret choosing this path? If so, she never expressed it except for one rare time—I was quite young and I think it related to a problem with one of my older brothers—when she burst into tears and said she shouldn't have had children. I still remember exactly where I was standing in the big farm kitchen and that one of my brothers was there, but I don't remember anything else about that moment. Nor do I have any memory of feeling unwanted, then or later, so I can only assume that she was able to work through whatever the issue was.

But my heart breaks for her now when I remember this. Was this a passing feeling of inadequacy in a particular situation, something many parents experience occasionally? Or did she carry this regret through her life? Did she dream of what could have been?

I watched my children learn to walk, then run, then head out into the world, praying they would find happiness. I was helpless when one suffered a bitter marriage breakup, and saddened when two of the five turned away from the spiritual beliefs so important to me. But they are all good and caring people. The oldest, who flew farthest from the nest, calls or writes weekly and one son and daughter-in-law nearby who drop in a few times a week. The other three visit often and take me to lunch or bring lunch to the home. They manoeuvre me into their vehicles and fold and load my wheelchair, then reverse the process when we get to my latest appointments with doctors or dentist or audiologist or optometrist, all which simply try to make my inevitable journey to the next world a little more comfortable. I miss knitting and reading and playing Scrabble; glasses can no longer correct my vision. I drop stitches, and words and Scrabble letter tiles blur.

> *Mom was not given to expansive emotions but the knives were out—very subtly—with Scrabble. She was deadly at playing strategic moves—and then shooting us a side "Gotcha" glance with a chuckle. "Mom," I said in one game, "you spoiled my 66 with a score of 15!" and she said, "Oh," so very sweetly, "I'm not sorry." We joked at her funeral that she must have seen no point in living when she could no longer play Scrabble in her last six months.*

Yesterday I revelled in the sound of the laughter of grandchildren who came for visits and chocolate chip cookies at Grandma's place. Today I catch only some of the words on the news or in a televised church service even with the earphones my children thought would help. My world is shrinking. I pray that my grandchildren and great-grandchildren find their way safely in what seems like a world with more violence and wars and hidden dangers and temptations.

> *My kids loved going to the farm, playing with the farm dog, cuddling farm kittens, visiting the sugar bush in maple syrup season, gathering fresh eggs from under the hens. I remember how both Mom and Dad delighted in holding their first great-grandchild, marvelling at the contrast between soft smooth baby skin and their own wrinkled skin.*

My good man is long gone after 57 years together, my life a solitary one in a room with a single bed with bars so I don't fall out in case I forget that I am no longer free to get out on my own.

> *We thought Mom, the quiet introvert in Dad's extrovert shadow, wouldn't long survive him but she displayed a steel core, living almost 19 years, on her own for the first 10 until a broken leg forced her into care. Even then, she enjoyed her small pleasures. Church services on TV, news and Jeopardy every night, knitting and reading, and simple treats like Timmie's coffee and a honey cruller much preferred to any upscale restaurant.*

Yesterday I was burying my parents, one so young at 55, the other at 82. Today, at 98, there is no one left to bury. My brother-in-law lost our bet as to which of us would last longer but, of course, I didn't collect anything except more useless time, four years and counting so far. So really, I lost the bet. And in those four years, I buried a son, an unnatural order in the scheme of life, a deep grief.

> *How I wish I couldn't relate to this, but I have also buried a child even though our grief journeys are different. Losing a child, a being you have known intimately from before birth, opens an emotional abyss. We differ in the ages, my daughter from an aneurysm at 30 after years of mental health struggles, my brother at 67 after a long illness. His illness and death were devastating—she said in a rare moment of sharing that this was her worst loss, worse than losing her husband.*

I look forward to meeting my Maker face to face. I've planned my funeral, chosen hymns and Scripture for the service and a plywood box strong enough to lower me into the ground beside my husband.

I weary of minutes and hours and days. I crave the release of the last sleep. I am tired to my core. So tired.

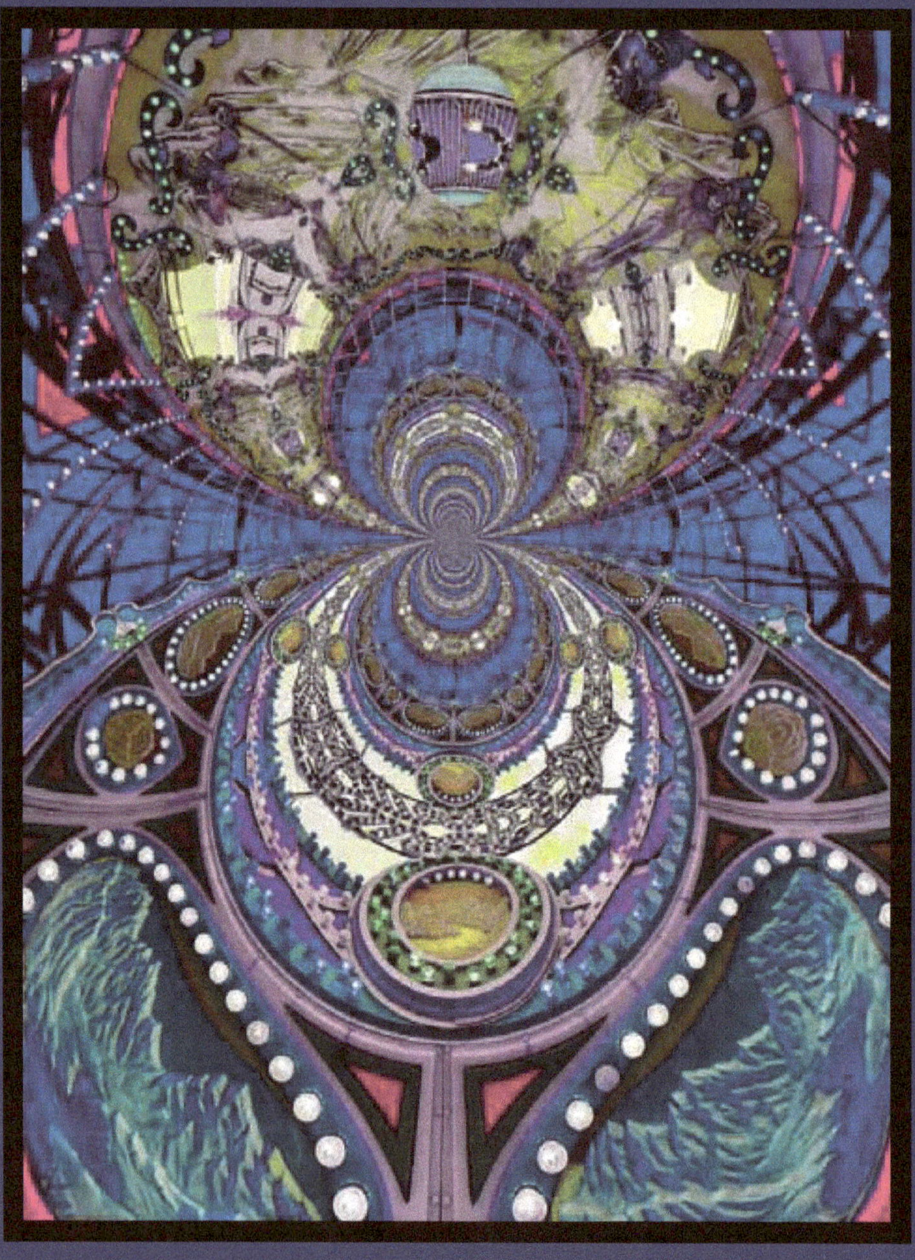

Midway Mandala Blue

Digital image by Marie-Lynn Hammond

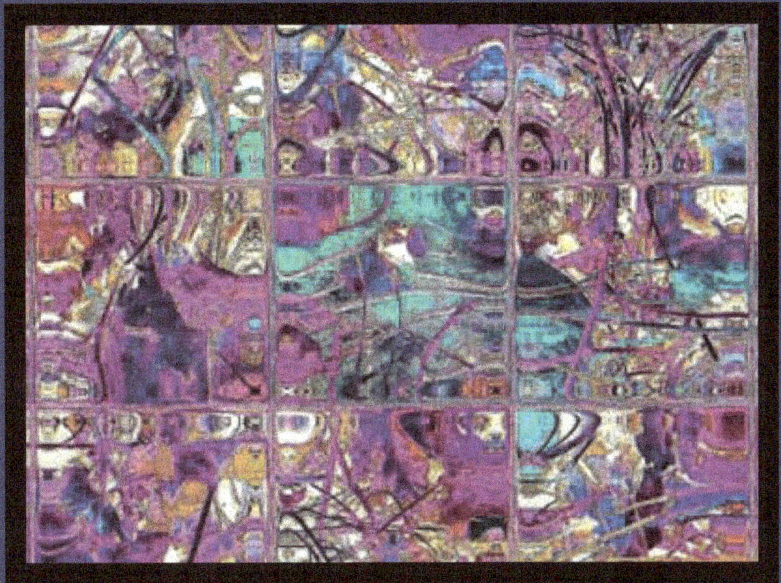

Emerald Pink

Digital image by Marie-Lynn Hammond

Kaleidostones

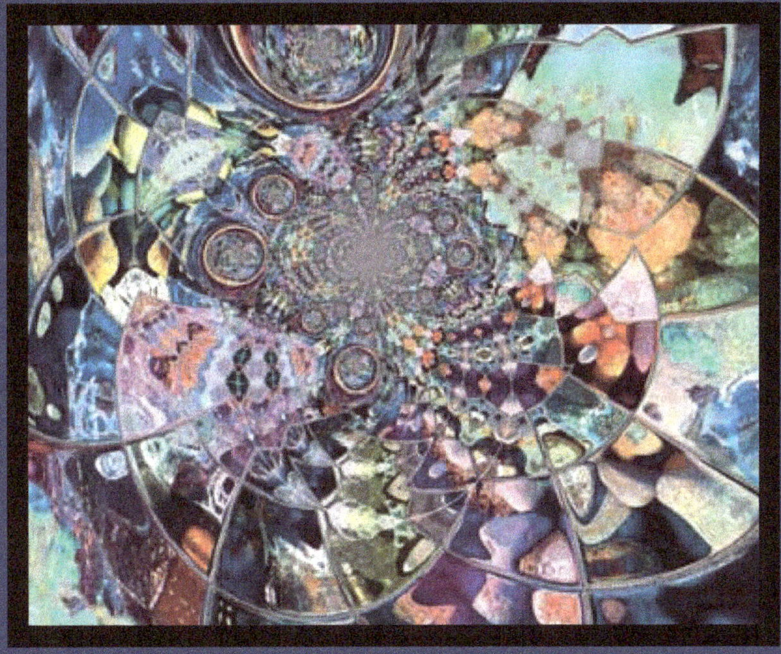

A Tribute to Don Gutteridge

September 30, 1937 – December 01, 2023

by John B. Lee

Now that the New Year is upon us, I can tell you that the thing I will miss the most in 2024 is my daily exchange of emails with Don Gutteridge. In that he was grieving over the loss of his grandson and of his wife Anne, and in that he was well into his eighties and weakened by ill health, he often contemplated in his poetry and in his emails the coming of his own death and thereby entering into that great mystery. In contemplating the considerable amount of poetry written about the mystery concerning what happens to individual consciousness when life comes to an end, and for those with the consolation of faith, and for those who like Don had lost their faith in youth, I reread some of Don's poetry this morning, and his poem "Body and Soul," on page 6 of *A Ground More Arable,* where he begins his poem "I'd like to think that some-/ where we are all immortal" and being painfully aware that I will not hear from Don again, though I can revisit his voice in the poems, I wrote the following elegy.

Poem Composed on the Death of a Friend

now my friend
your dictionary settles into silence
and your music
quiets in the ink
the song has ended
with a final heartbeat
and a fatal breath
somewhere it seems
you've learned
the lessons of the soul
the time has come
the hour that stills the movement
of the hand
and quells the voice
how many moments

in speculative language
you wondered at the mystery
upon the threshold of belief
as with a stranger's awe
you came to know there's ghost work
in the doing now
like every poet from the past
you dreamed an unborn reader
with a finger drawn to fix the eye
upon a sentient line
composed in contemplation
of that cognitive loss
where the dread of nothing
lingers for the faithless
as you moved into the gloom that steals the mind
to mark
a dark parenthesis
of unseen light

John B. Lee

I belong to a writing group that meets at the art centre in Simcoe once a month on the first Thursday of each month. Each attendee shares a recent piece of writing. In January I chose to read my elegy "Poem Composed on the Death of a Friend." In that this poem is an homage to my good friend Don Gutteridge, I included a poem of his from his collection *A Ground More Arable (Wet Ink Books, 2023)*. Don's poem "Body-and-Soul" is an exemplary contemplation of his own mortality. This poem is all the more poignant because it appears in a signed volume of the last collection of poems I received from Don. These words appearing on the title page in Don's blue ink script "For John with affection & best wishes." Neither he nor I were aware of the poignancy of those words at the time, so I cherish the imaginary movement of his hand and those words written in the wake of his living pen. Sadly, I shall never receive such a salutation ever again. Here is Don's poem:

Body-and-Soul

I'd like to think that some-
where we are all immortal
in a place where the good gods
grin and forgive, where some
semblance of what we once were,
abides and breathes, a sanctuary
for the solace of souls, where we can
recall everything we've un-
remembered, and those we loved
till our bones bled and surrendered
to Death's dominion, bind up
our wounds, and even though
we may believe in Heaven's
leavening or the gift of grace,
body-and-soul will find
a way to come uncoupled
and grieve on their own.

Don Gutteridge

I had the privilege of sharing the pages with Don Gutteridge in two books. The first was an homage to our fathers which I edited for publication by Black Moss Press in 2022. I invited Richard (Tai) Grove and Don Gutteridge to submit poems on the theme of Fathers. I chose to call the collection, *Fathers & Sons*, borrowing that title from a novel by Russian author Ivan Turgenev. Don called his contribution "He Soared on Wings the Ice Only Gave to the Young." Don often wrote about hockey, and in so doing he wrote poems in praise of his father who had been a very talented player. Here is an excerpt from a section of a longer poem "Good Will":

iii

the papers said
they couldn't build
a rink big enough
to swallow your pride

My dad on skates and
over ice that was
ground, a gravity
giving speed, a
moving not of its own
but a boy on blades
making wings out of
legs   arms the heart
swelling thru every
muscle drew order
out of energy
design from the
chaos of the game

with a stick held
like a brand
he burned the puck
beyond the net
the circling boards
the crowd's containment
beyond the
            perfection of applause
he soared on wings
the ice gave only
to the young and once ...

Don Gutteridge

On another occasion Don and I collaborated on a collection published by
Hidden Brook Press in 2020. I chose the title *By & By* for this collaboration
as a pun thereby acknowledging that some of the poems were by yours truly,
and some by Don. As an epigram for this collection, I chose the lines from
the eponymous hymn "In the Sweet By and By." The opening verse of the
song are particularly poignant because so many of the poems in Don's
section relate to the loss of his wife Anne and to the untimely passing of his
grandson Tom. In the preface to the anthology, I wrote "We have become
something of a mutual admiration society. We correspond frequently. He
sends me his new poems, and I send him mine. We communicate on dozens
of topics. We share a belief in the importance of keeping the faith in
poetry."

I ended the preface by signing off with these words:

"However, despite the reference to the afterlife, I assure you that both Don Gutteridge and I are very much alive, and this won't be the last time you hear from us." Sadly, this is a fond fare the well. That said, I conclude this piece by choosing one of Don's poems on one of his favourite themes, not an elegy, not a morbid reminder of mortality, not a lamentation on the loss of a friend or a loved one, all of which are frequent themes of Don's poems, but rather an erotic celebration of joie de vivre, a celebration of youthful awakening of his very masculine fascination with and appreciation of the girls of his youth.

Hallelujah

When Shirley McCord was still
almost-a-woman, I willed
the bottle to spin her way
and was more than satisfied
at a winning smile, and later
in the day, jumping rope,
she raised her leg so high
I cried Hallelujah
and praised the Lord.

Don Gutteridge

Words for Don Gutteridge

by Miguel Ángel Olivé Igelsia

One of the greatest, most impressive literary luminaries of the endless Canadian cultural mosaic has passed away, Donald (Don) Gutteridge. What words, what phrases would best honour him? What attitudes and acts would best pay tribute to an author who could not stop writing and whose legacy is amongst the most fertile, solid ones in Canada? Let´s ponder these questions and find the most fitting answers so we stand up and salute such fine writer and human being.

An understanding of the significance of Canadian poet Don Gutteridge may start by reading the following: "*Literary critics will have much to say about Gutteridge's uniquely Canadian vision. I am content that his poetry is accessible, unobtrusive, delights the ear, stirs the heart and even enters into the soul. It is the art that mirrors inner life*". These are the words of R. G. Moyles (The University of Alberta. In The Journal of Canadian Poetry).

The first part tells us of a "*unique Canadian vision*". Hallelujah. Gutteridge was one of those gifted people who grasped with mastery the Canadian concept, maximizing it and manifesting it in their writings. Read his poem "Dunes at Canatara" about which I said was *Purdian* in spirit:

> It took a million years
> to sculpt these dunes,
> grain by grain of wavewashed sand whipped
> by seasoned winds into
> voluptuous curves
> and bevelled runes.
> It took my pals and me
> an afternoon to put
> our imprimatur upon
> the shimmering concavities,
> our bodies pressing
> their wry signatures deep
> deep into the sun-stunned sand,
> feeling the heat of a hundred
> centuries oozing through.

The second part of Moyles's quote tells us of the quality and characteristics of his poetry: *"accessible, unobtrusive, delights the ear, stirs the heart and even enters into the soul."* Moyles is pointing out the ease with which readers can enter and walk through Gutteridge's poetry.

Nothing will stand in the way between them and the poet, no inextricable paths, no obscure rhetoric, no jumbled, superfluous overdoing of line and meaning. Beyond that, features that define outstanding poetry in English – rhythm, which is ear-comforting, power, which is heart-reaching– are revealed by Moyles. Finally, the feature that makes a poet just one more poet or a transcendent one, like him: Gutteridge's poetry *"enters the soul."* Once we read his work, it will unequivocally win our hearts and settle in our deepest recesses reserved for great things, those that move the spirit and enlighten us. Enjoy the poems below, where Don summed up his connection with poetry:

Rhymes

In my advancing age
let me still be the one
wrestling with words to wield
the world anew, to send
them dancing on some
distant dais, sylvan
with simile: the page
where all my rhymes ring
true.

Ruthless

And me composing poems:
inklings I tease
towards some sense
in words whetted upon
the wheel of memory
and swerving askance
upon the page where they lean
upright, enlinked,
ready to be swallowed whole,
raw and ruthless
in rhythmic pursuit
of the truth.

But it was Don himself who exposed his own poet's soul when he said to me in response to a question I asked him: "*Nothing short of a stroke could stop me from writing poetry… I seem to dream poems and wake up writing them… I am very fortunate that the Muse has never let me down.*" He said that for my book *Five Canadian Poets* (QuodSermo Publishing, 2021), and proved his deep bond with poetry as I delved into his life and work and wrote *The Canadian Poet Who Wrote Himself Whole* (QuodSermo Publishing, 2022) in honor to his long-standing career.

Writing about Don, especially the latter book, which was entirely about him, I knew it meant a huge undertaking but a necessary and meaningful one. There is an unobjectionably literary, educational, tasteful, evocative, kindhearted and elegant value in what Don wrote. His oeuvre is an invaluable contribution to literature, a treasure in Canadian literary heritage.

I have said before that Don Gutteridge had a singular style, comfortably placed within a latent universality. He was recipient, repository and paradigm at the same time. He was committed to his land, evidenced when we read his poems and notice references to nature, to geographies and seasons, to vast maps of wildlife and wilderness.

In Gutteridge, there was an unavoidable, deeply-ingrained family-friend-wife leitmotif. About his family poems, Emily-Jane Hills Orford said, "*Special family connections. The simplicity of treasured family moments…*" (Hidden Brook Press release). She added, "*I have read a number of Don Gutteridge's poems over the years and I continue to marvel at his ability to capture the simplest of moments in a capsule and make it grander than life with his poetic observations.*" (ibidem) Read "Together":

> In this photo, my mother
> and father, standing tall
> on my grandfather's lawn
> in their Sunday suits,
> hold me up high
> between them for the camera's
> loving eye, like a prized
> doll for all the world
> to see, their hands tethered
> to steady me on my maiden
> shoot, as happy as they
> will ever be, and I still
> regret I wasn't enough
> to keep them together

I have often stated that *"Canadian poets excel in wording, honoring and recalling facts, events, people, and names."* Don's poems invariably state whom they were written for. Particularly moving are the ones written to Anne, his wife, and to Tom, his grandson. Even though sadness was present in the cry of the bereaved man, Don found consolation in beauty and memories. The poet did not complain or lament forever: he saw a form of healing in writing. Imagery pulses and emanates from Don's poetry; he handled language tools fruitfully, innovatively. An essential component of the poet's poetry is the link of rhythm and musicality. Both elements were unavoidable for him, as he also told me while I was writing my aforementioned books.

One stunning example of his love for Anne, his wife, is "Au Revoir." It is a heart-breaking poem. We see a sophisticated poet in love, deeply in love for his departed wife. Everything reminded him of her. Torn in pain and nostalgia, he wove scene after scene, image after image, glued to the physicality of her memory. Despite grief, he managed to erect a monumental piece here and in other poems, *"elegies for my beloved wife,"* as he told me once:

> I do not empty this house
> of your presence: you are here
> in every room we shared
> breath in, your clothes still
> hang where they belong
> in their closets, and every painting
> that adorns our walls is a reminder
> of your artist's eye, and the chesterfield,
> your bête noir, still
> bears your imprint, and a novel
> lies where your fingers last
> lingered, nor am I made
> forlorn on entering the space
> now vacant of the woman
> I cossetted and cradled with
> love in its essence, for we are taught
> that death is not an ending,
> not goodbye but au revoir:
> I refuse that platitude,
> preferring your haunting hover
> and the remnants of the things you touched
> with such tenderness.

In all his greatness as a poet and person, Gutteridge was a modest human being. Alongside many other Canadian contemporary writers, Gutteridge has left a mark on what I termed in my book *Five Canadian Poets* as <u>the Canadian style</u>.

Gutteridge belongs with those iconic writers who dignify the Canadian literary mosaic, who are a part of, as John B. Lee puts it, the *"Great literature"* [that] *"broadens our knowledge, deepens our understanding, clarifies our emotions, and connects us to the inner wells of the self where deep need is served. In great literature we also find a meaningful connection with our fellow humans."*

Don Gutteridge's writings expand our cognition and understanding of the world, shake and set our own emotions free, and activate our nexuses with ourselves and our innermost urges. Moreover, his poetry comes from his connection with human beings and helps us revisit our own, substantially, indelibly, transcendently. As Christian Sia of Readers' Favorite observed, *"These poems are filled with the humanity of the writer and readers can easily relate to the emotions evoked in the lines…"* (Hidden Brook Press release)

If at the beginning of these words I suggested readers to start with Moyles's quotation, now I include a longer critique by John B. Lee, in reference to one of Don's books, which condenses Gutteridge's immeasurable quality as a writer: *"I read poem after poem and think it is a masterpiece. There is an abiding sadness, but the sadness of wisdom, of knowing that if we live long enough, we lose loved ones, we keep them in our hearts though they are gone. Long ago I coined the phrase "the presence of absence" to capture in as few words as possible what I felt when I thought of those loved ones I'd lost. We preserve them in poems. We keep them alive in memory and dream. We weep and grieve and lament and celebrate. This book is profound and wise and consoling. I will be reading it again and again because it goes deep. It has the courage of autobiography without the honey trap of the confessional."* (Hidden Brook Press release)

Gutteridge never ceased to write and wonder at the world inside and outside him. Only Death made him pause—yet we have the vastness of his oeuvre. He was always caught up in the mystery that is putting words and sentences together to create something that was, to him, indefinable. Read "Unsayable":

> I've spent a lifetime
> seeking the reason for rhyme
> in pursuit of the perfect poem
> where dactyls dance until
> they make indelible sense
> in the midst of metrical meaning,

where I find my heart stirred
by the motive for metaphor
in the ept uttering of the un-
word, the saying of what is,
alas, unsayable.

There we go, Don Gutteridge's poetry is invincible ink and *"indelible sense"*. I invite everyone to toast to the man, the husband, the family man, the father, the friend, the writer, the symbol—the bard. Let's close these comments about Don with precisely a poem he titled "Bard":

I find it hard to imagine
a life without the wizardry
of words: the nuances of nouns
and verbs surging: pinned
in the prism of a poem, where rhyme
has its reasons and rhythm is what
the heart hears in the silence
between beats and simile
has its seasons, and I was born
to pain and poetry, and longed
to embrace the arcane business
of being a bard.

We have been deprived of the physical presence of a great, but his aura, his transcendence, his profound spirituality will accompany us. His books and his legacy are intact, invincible. Thank you, Don…

I begged permission from Devour´s editor, Richard Grove, to finish with a poem I wrote for Don when I learned about his demise. May it be my humble tribute to his life and work:

Requiem for Don

… love is again begun and olden souls reborn… Don Gutteridge
… and make you mine again. Don Gutteridge
To Don Gutteridge, in memoriam
December 2023

Death did not take you, Don:
You decided to cross the threshold
towards the place where Anne
had been waiting for you
all these past years. You never
ceased to regale her with showers
of poems; you never stopped
letting your readers know
how much you loved her,
how much you missed her.
Death has been conquered instead,
the romance has been kept alive
and metaphors have pulsed eternally ablaze…
Now, you decided it was time
to read Anne your poems
face to face, show her—lost in her
blue eyes—all the passion
and the loyalty you professed
as the moment to be reunited
finally arrived.
Death did not take you, Don:
you simply chose to go.
Your faithful readers
bid you farewell celebrating
your renewed journey besides Anne.

Miguel Ángel Olivé Igelsia

Words for Don Gutteridge, a Friend and Fellow Poet

By Richard Grove

In the quiet passing of December 01, 2023, the world of Canadian literature mourned the loss of a true luminary, a dear friend, and a poetic virtuoso, Don Gutteridge, the Prince of Canadian Poetry. For years I had virtually daily contact with Don about his poetry, literary prose and academic writing. His passing has left a hole in my heart. As he gracefully inched toward 90, Don left an indelible mark on the literary landscape of Canada, earning the affection and admiration of fellow poets, writers, and literature enthusiasts.

Don Gutteridge's legacy transcends mere ink on paper; it intertwines with the very fabric of Canadian literary history. Often hailed as the modern Canadian William Shakespeare, he possessed an extraordinary ability to weave words into tapestries of emotion and insight that resonated with readers across generations. His poetry, rich with the essence of the Canadian experience, often painted memoiresk, landscapes of his youth and family life. His themes often included loving tributes to his late grandson Tom and his late wife Anne, expressing intricate nuances of the human soul.

Beyond the accolades and titles, Don Gutteridge's contribution to CanLit was a labour of love, a prolific commitment that surpassed the passing trends of literary fashion. His body of work, over 70 titles, is a testament to a lifetime dedicated to the craft, is a cherished treasury for those nourished in his pages of poetry. The beauty of his words and the depth of his themes have earned him a permanent residence in the hearts of Canadian poets and lit-lovers alike.

In the vast expanse of eternity, Don Gutteridge's legacy will endure. His poems will echo in the minds of those who seek the profound and the sublime in the written word. As we bid farewell to the Prince of Canadian Poetry, we are left not with sorrow but with gratitude for the gift of his talent and the lasting impact of his pen. Don Gutteridge's love for writing, his commitment to the craft, and the beauty he infused into every line have ensured that he is not lost to time but survives in perpetuity, a poetic beacon guiding the way for future generations of Canadian wordsmiths.

Dear Don, you are missed by many.

Let me share these three poems dedicated to his beloved wife Anne. All three poems were included in Don's most recent book *Gilding the Lily*, published by Wet Ink Books, released just before his passing. Sadly, Don never had the fortune of holding this book in his hands. This makes me sad but let's rejoice in knowing that Don was writing poems up to his last days. All three poems are memoiresk in content and style.

Where it Would

December-January:1960-61
For Anne in fond memory

When I finally got up enough
nerve to give you a kiss
with full-lipped zip
and our tongues tangled in twinned
vim, you happened to mention
you weren't a fan of animate
osculation, and so thereafter
we nibbled lobes or nudged
noses (like fur-blurred Innuit
keeping their igloo juiced)
or hugged like siblings at a
family fête, letting
love bloom where it would
in the parked dark.

Newborn

For Anne in fond memory

If I were one of the good
gods controlling the cosmos,
I'd enshrine you as a star in a
far-flung, filigreed
curve of the firmament or as a
moon, lit by its own
self-rinsing glow, but I am
just a word-starved bard
who has not lustre enough
to limn your loveliness or beatify
your beauty, but wherever you be,
in the star-fractured dark
or harbouring the newborn
illume of a moon, I'll send you
my love and embark on the next
body-bruising cruise
to your inner-galactic grotto
and make you mine again.

Breathless

For Anne in fond memory

When I have reached my God allotted
days, I'll save
my dying breath to blow you
the poem I've been penning
since the time I first lay
my loving eyes on yours,
not a sonnet, whose rhyme encrusted
quatrains could not
encompass the beauty you bore
with such a winning grace,
nor a brave-heart ballad
that might catch something
of our stirring story but not
enough, and though I've composed
a dozen beguiling odes
to the way you let your eyes
do the smiling, I find that,
in the end, only an epic
would suffice with room to limn
your loveliness, but then, when God
has called my body home,
I'll have no need of words,
or thought, or breath to blow you
a perfect poem.

I am so delighted with all three poems. For me, the poem "Where it Would" reflects a moment of intimacy, capturing the tension between desire and the hesitations of the other person, Anne. Don, the narrator, recounts a kiss that reveals vulnerability and courage, yet it's met with the realization that the other person may not share the same enthusiasm for such expressions of affection. The poet then describes a subtle shift in their physical interactions, choosing more modest gestures like nibbling lobes or nudging noses. The phrase "letting love bloom where it would" suggests a willingness to adapt and find beauty in unconventional expressions of love. The poem explores the dynamics of intimacy and the various forms it can take, ultimately settling into a tender acceptance.

In the poem "Newborn" Don takes on a cosmic and mythological tone, imagining the subject as a celestial entity. The poet expresses a desire to immortalize the beloved, either as a star or a moon. The use of imagery like "far-flung, filigreed curve of the firmament" creates a sense of vastness and beauty. However, the poet acknowledges their limitations as a mere "word-starved bard" incapable of fully capturing the beloved's beauty. Despite this, there's a commitment to sending love across cosmic distances. The poem blends celestial imagery with personal emotion, creating a unique perspective on love and the desire for the beloved to shine eternally.

And finally, with the poem "Breathless" Don contemplates the end of their life and envisions a poetic gesture towards the beloved. The choice of saving the last breath to blow a poem to the loved one adds a poignant layer to the narrative. The poet grapples with the inadequacy of traditional poetic forms to encapsulate the depth of the beloved's beauty. The poem references sonnets, ballads, and odes, suggesting that these conventional forms fall short. The desire for an epic poem speaks to the grandiosity of the emotions involved. The closing lines convey a sense of acceptance that, in the end, words may be insufficient to encapsulate the depth of their love, and the perfect poem is left as an unattainable ideal.

For me it is wonderful how these three poems collectively explore different facets of love, from the nuanced dynamics of intimacy to celestial and cosmic metaphors. This is all so typical of Don's breadth of expression as a poet. These personal and poignant undertones are characteristic throughout *Gilding the Lily*, adding depth and emotional resonance to the entire book. As publisher and friend I am proud to bring this book to the world.

Richard M. Grove / Tai

Anna Yin
anna.yin@gmail.com

Music never stops

For Don

So now you are in heaven
the great mystery
where ink never dries
and music never stops
No more in a solitary room
nor a long night
but abundant light and height
and the ceiling is your floor
No more a frail body
nor coughing
but dancing steps
to your loved ones
to meet the fine writers
and great sages before us
with final peace and joy
The starlight tapestry you left behind
will brighten us in this world
We will cherish each of your parting gifts

Note: *It was my honour to translate Don's poetry
and publish Starlight Tapestry in 2023*

A Biography Excerpt from,
The Perilous Journey of Gavin the Great
Wet Ink Books 2023

by Kimberley E. Grove

Don Gutteridge started his writing career when he was confined to his bed for nine months with rheumatic fever when he should have been enjoying Grade 2. Don was never lazy so he read enough books to fill his imagination and learn the craft of writing. When he returned to school in Grade 3 he wrote a story for his teacher Miss McDonald. She praised it so much that he realized he was on to something. And he has been writing ever since.

He has published 45 poetry books, 13 novels, 12 mysteries and 11 non-fiction books, as well as numerous articles. In his own words he talks about the thrill of his first published poem in a respected literary magazine, *The Fiddlehead.* "In the Fall of 1960, my wife Anne and I, both starting to teach that month in the Elmira High School, and decided to live in the nearby village of Elora. We moved into the servants' quarters of the old George Drew homestead and began our married life. I now made a life-changing decision. Having had poems published in the Western's literary magazine, I decided I would start sending the few new short lyrics I was writing to *The Fiddlehead* poetry magazine, edited by Professor Fred Cogswell. Tucking several poems into my case, I walked to the local post office (there was no mail delivery in the village) and, both thrilled and fearful, I mailed the poems to be judged, not by student editors, but by some literary man or woman of taste, 2000 miles away. Every morning for two months, I walked into the village square to check my mail. I watched the leaves go gold and crimson and finally fall and drift. There was no response to my maiden gambit. I felt crestfallen and began to regret announcing to Anne that I was planning to become a published poet. Sometime in the chill of November, there was a letter for me, my own self-addressed envelope. I let it sit on the kitchen table awhile and, when Anne was abroad, found the courage to open it. One of my poems had been accepted, a six-line fragment I had been debating sending, but with it a short note in Professor Cogswell's scrawl, to say the poem would be published in the Spring edition of the magazine. I was a published poet on my first try. And thus began a fifty-year relationship with Fred Cogswell, a luminary of our literary world. Within three years, he would publish three of the mid-length narrative poems I had begun to write and, in 1968, my first published book, *Riel*. I was no longer an apprentice. That Autumn of 1960 was one of the seminal experiences of my life." The *Riel* book was such a masterpiece that CBC picked up on the genius of the writing and did a radio drama of it.

There were quite a few stories in Don's own history that prove the saying, "Life is stranger than fiction." His maternal grandmother, Lilly Smith, met his grandfather in Detroit. She had been married once before. "When she was sixteen, her father wagered her in a craps game, lost and handed his daughter over to a William Campbell, whom she was forced to marry." Campbell abandoned her when Roy Campbell was born, so she divorced him.

"My maternal grandfather (John McWatters, a.resident of Sarnia, Ontario) worked as a carpenter until he retired in the Spring of 1939. He worked at odd jobs, and one day after finishing a job and being paid, he headed straight to his regular bootleggers, where he partied with friends well into the night. Sometime towards morning he stepped onto the porch of the house for a smoke and was struck viciously from behind. Unconscious, he collapsed face-down in the garden. Too inebriated to move his head, he suffocated and died there. The inquest, written up in lurid detail in *The Sania Observer*, concluded that my grandfather was murdered by a person or persons unknown. The coroner said he had never heard such lying in a courtroom." In addition to Don's mother, Grace, Don's Uncle George was born into the McWatters' family.

"Uncle George was a brilliant man. At age twenty-five he was CEO of a Detroit bakery. Unfortunately, he had the McWatters gambling instinct. While working in Detroit he got tangled up with the local mob. Nothing happened until a few years later, when he had married and returned to Sarnia, and raised two sons. He began working for the Sarnia City Bus Company as a bus driver. He was given the Point Edward route and while waiting at the terminal two blocks from my home, he would ask me to get on, feed me peanuts, drive around the block and let me off. Within a short time, he became president of the company. At the same time, he got into the debt of the Detroit mob, who threatened to break his legs if he did not pay up. Desperate, he embezzled the money from the company, paid the mob, but was caught when the books were examined. They thought so highly of him, that he was not charged, merely let go. He vowed never to gamble again, but as gambling was all he had left, he set up a gambling den (illegal at that time) above the Cozy Café in Sarnia, dealt the cards (to the higher ups in the Refinery and Polymer plant and other respectable bigwigs) and took five per cent of the pot. His wife, my Aunt Grace, made and served the sandwiches. I heard about Aunt Grace but never saw her in those days because, ill with some mysterious ailment (depression likely) she took to her bed for two years and never left it. I finally met her in the 1960s when she and Uncle George came to London to visit my mother."

Uncle George who married a Grace, the same name as his sister, had a son Dick when they were living in Detroit, but they moved to Canada shortly after but never mentioned to their son that he was born in the United States. One night in 1951 when Dick was in Port Huron, Michigan, enjoying the night life, he was stopped at the border by Customs and told that his draft number had come up and he was sent immediately to Korea.. "Dick served in Korea for a year and a half in the thick of the fighting. When he returned he was a changed man. He never married."

Some of these stories made it into Don's writing with some poetic license. In addition, he used his father figure for the main character of his first novel, Bus-Ride. His father (William Ernest Charles Gutteridge) was an excellent hockey player, well- known in Southern Ontario, and scouted by the Detroit Red Wings. However, in those early days of hockey, the players weren't paid like they are today and instead of playing hockey for a living, he signed up with the Royal Canadian Air Force (RCAF). During some of his years of service, the family lived in an apartment above the grandparents in Point Edward (a village near Sarnia) just across the border from the United States. If a person can fall in love with a place, then Don did just that. Much of his writing was based in Point Edward and the people he knew there. His father had moved the family away from the village to Sarnis Township when he finished his time in the RCAF. "The move into the lonely countryside, away from my home village, was devastating for me. For two years my brother and I, every second week, walked to the train station and caught the bus to Point Edward, where we stayed with Gran and Gramps, and tried to keep up the fraying friendships that had been so much a part of my life." The other hardship of his life was his disconnect with his father. "We had a difficult time bonding: he was a superb athlete, I wasn't." His father was away so much that eventually he left the family and moved to Calgary where he got work as a taxidermist. His parents divorced and his father also started to drink heavily which eventually killed him.) The main character of Don's first apprentice novel was based on his father. He sent his book to Jack McClelland who liked it, but was concerned that the entire book had not one word of dialogue. He went on to learn that aspect of his craft when Alice Munro explained that dialogue comes naturally from the creation of strong characters put in the same room.

Don's Dad then moved the family to Chatham, Ontario. After studying at Chatham Collegiate Institute, he was accepted in 1956 to the University of Western Ontario where he received an Honours Degree in English Language and Literature. Following that, he had the opportunity to teach English to students at the Grades 11, 12 and 13 level at Elmira District High School. In addition to realizing that he had found a profession that he loved, he also met the woman of his dreams, Margaret Anne Barnett, the Home Economics teacher. "I proposed on a snowy night in February 1961 in Anne's new Volkswagon. We were married by a judge in Guelph and attended a small reception for us by school friends and my mother and brother. We rented the back half (servant's quarters) of a big house (the old Drew homestead) and began our married life, driving each day from Elora to Elmira District High School. Many weekends we drove to Toronto for musicals and plays at the O'Keefe Centre. It was a wonderful winter and spring. Over 85% of my Grade 13 students passed their provincial English exam."

In 1963 his work on a M.A. was halted because he realized that he needed to obtain employment to support his newborn son, William John Barnett Gutteridge. His daughter, Catherine Anne Gutteridge, was born in 1966. Family life was a blessing as it gave him the opportunity to see a lot of Canada as they enjoyed family outings and camping.

He returned to his passion of teaching at Beck Collegiate in London. This work led to his teaching English Methods to prospective High School teachers for 25 years at Althouse, which became a Faculty of Education at University of Western Ontario. It is easy to see that his love of teaching benefited his students, too, as he still is in contact with some of them today. He also wrote 10 academic books that will undoubtedly help others that share his love of teaching.

Bored with retirement, he wrote a twelve-volume mystery series, *The Marc Edwards Mysteries*, with four publishers over a twelve-year period (2003-2015). This engaged him with his other favourite subject, History, as these books creatively cover the story of an ensign, Marc Edwards, from 1836-1841. They describe Canada in a way that is easy to digest for anyone interested in that period of our country's history, as he did a great deal of research to get the facts correct about the times, although his main character is fictional.

When Don talks about the special moments in his life, he refers to his children's births and the wonderful marriage he shared with Anne. His joy extends from his grandparents to his six grandchildren. This book is dedicated to Tom, the grandchild that lived with him and Anne for six years and dedicated a large amount of time to reading and talking about his grandfather's works.

Tom created several podcasts (https://thereandthen.podbean.com/) in which the public can learn more about Don's thought process when writing. You can hear the enjoyment Don had in doing the interviews. At some points, you hear his laughter when talking about his characters, as though he gets as much enjoyment from them as his reader will.

"It's been a full life." And the list of his works that follows is proof of that:

Poetry

Riel: A Poem For Voices. Fiddlehead Poetry Books: Fredericton, 1968; and Van Nostrand Reinhold: Toronto, 1972.

The Village Within. Fiddlehead: Fredericton, 1970.

Death At Quebec and Other Poems. Fiddlehead: Fredericton, 1971.

"Perspectives: Poems Toward a Biography." Pennywise Press, London, Ontario, 1971.

Saying Grace: An Elegy. Fiddlehead: Fredericton, 1972.

Coppermine: The Quest For North. Oberon: Ottawa, 1973.

Borderlands. Oberon: Ottawa, 1975.

Tecumseh. Oberon: Ottawa, 1976.

A True History of Lambton County. Oberon: Ottawa, 1977.

God's Geography. Brick Books: London, 1982.

The Exiled Heart; Selected Narratives. Oberon: Ottawa, 1986.

Love in the Wintertime. Oberon: Ottawa, 1990.

Flute Music in the Cello's Belly. Moonstone: Goderich, 1997.

Bloodlines. Oberon: Ottawa, 2001.

Something More Miraculous. Oberon: Ottawa, 2004.

Still Magical. Oberon: Ottawa, 2007.

Coming Home. Oberon: Ottawa, 2011.

The Way It Was. Friesen Press: Vancouver, 2014.

Tidings. Black Moss Press: Windsor, 2015.

Peripheries. (ebook) First Choice Books: Victoria, 2016.

Inundations. Hidden Brook Press: Brighton, 2016.

The Blue Flow Below. Black Moss Press: Windsor, 2017.

"The Sands of Canatara " (ebook) First Choice Books: Victoria, 2017.

"Inklings" Black Moss Press: Windsor, 2017.

"The Village Within" (re-issue, ebook)) First Choice Books: Victoria, 2017.

"Cameron Lake" (ebook) First Choice Books: Victoria, 2018.

"Home Ground" Hidden Brook Press, 2018.

"Two Dozen for Anne, First Choice books, Victoria, 2018

"Bereft: Poems for my Beloved," First Choice Books, Victoria, 2018.

"Another Poem For Anne," First Choice Books, Victoria, 2018.

"Days Worth the Telling," Black Moss Press, Windsor, 2018.

"The Breath of My Being," First Choice Books, Victoria, 2018.
"Foster's Pond," Borealis, Ottawa, 2019
"The Star-Brushed Horizon,' Hidden Brook Press, 2019.
"Mara's Lamp," Black Moss Press. 2019.
"Impious Whims: Selected Poems." Borealis Press, 2019.
"In the Rarefied Regions of the Heart". Hidden Brook Press, 2020.
"Point Taken: Collected Poems 2014-2020." Hidden Brook Press, 2020.
"By and By". With John B. Lee. Hidden Brook Press 2020.
"The Derelict Heart". Hidden Brook Press: 2020.
"Invincible Ink." Hidden Brook Press, 2020.
"Into the Milkweed Meadow." Hidden Brook Press, 2021.
"Where Rivers Run Deep." Hidden Brook Press, 2021
"More Boding Than Blood." Hidden Brook Press, 2021.
"The Ardent Dark," Hidden Brook Press, 2021.
"Going for the Grail" Wet Ink Books, 2022
"Lover's Moon", Wet Ink Books, 2022
"The Home We Never Leave" Wet Ink Books, 2022
"Death at Quebec" Wet Ink Books, 2022
"Trawling for Truth" Wet Ink Books, 2022
"Kingdom Come" Wet Ink Books, 2022
"A Goat Footed Dance" Wet Ink Books, 2022
"A Fine-Tuned Heart" Wet Ink Books, 2023
"O Frabjous Day!" Wet Ink Books, 2023
"A Ground More Arable" Wet Ink Books, 2023
"Sailing with the Wind" Wet Ink Books, 2023
"Bumper Crop 01" Wet Ink Books, 2023
"Bumper Crop 02" Wet Ink Books, 2023
"Gilding the Lily" Wet Ink Books – December 2023 (*This was Don's last book just before his passing. Don was writing right up until his last days*)

Fiction

Bus-Ride. Nairn publishing: Nairn, 1974.
All in Good Time. Black Moss: Windsor, 1980.
St. Vitus Dance. Drumlin: London, 1986.
Shaman's Ground. Drumlin: London, 1988.
How the World Began. Moonstone: Goderich, 1991.
Summer's Idyll. Oberon: Ottawa, 1993.
Winter's Descent. Oberon: Ottawa, 1996.
Bewilderment. Borealis: Ottawa, 2000.
The Perilous Journey of Gavin the Great. Borealis Press: Ottawa, 2010.
The Rebellion Mysteries. Simon and Schuster: Toronto, 2012.
Lily's Story.(e-book). Bev Editions: Toronto, 2013 (Print edition 2014)
Constable Garrett and the Dead Ringer. Tellwell: Victoria, 2016
"Lily Fairchild," Tablo publications, 2019

"The Perilous Journey of Gavin the Great" 2022
"The Perilous Journey of Gavin the Great" Illustrated 2nd Edtion 2023

Marc Edwards Mysteries
Turncoat. McClelland and Stewart: Toronto, 2003.
Solemn Vows. McClelland and Stewart: Toronto, 2003.
Vital Secrets. Trinity: Saint John, 2007.
Dubious Allegiance. Simon and Schuster: Toronto, 2012.
Bloody Relations. Simon and Schuster: Toronto, 2013.
Death of a Patriot. Simon and Schuster: Toronto, 2014.
The Bishop's Pawn. Tablo Publishing: Melbourne, 2021
Desperate Acts. Tablo Publishing: Melbourne, 2021
Unholy Alliance. Tablo Publishing: Melbourne, 2021.
"Mnor Corruption *Tablo Publishing: Melbourne, 2021*
Governing Passion Tablo Publishing: Melbourne, 2021
The Widow's Demise Tablo Publishing: Melbourne, 2021.
The six mysteries above were also published as ebooks by Bev Editions in 2015.

Non-Fiction
Rhetoric: A Unified Approach to Literary Curricula. OISE: Toronto, 1970 (contributor)
Language and Expression. McClelland and Stewart: Toronto, 1970.
The Country of the Young. The Althouse Press: London, 1978.
Mountain and Plain. Anthology. McClelland and Stewart: Toronto, 1978.
Rites of Passage. Anthology. McClelland and Stewart: Toronto, 1979.
Brave Season. The Althouse Press: London, 1983.
Incredible Journeys. The Althouse Press: London, 1986 and 1990.
The Dimension of Delight. The Althouse Press: London, 1988.
Stubborn Pilgrimage. Our Schools/Our Selves: Toronto, 1994.
Teaching English. Lorimer: Toronto, 2000.
The Myth Alive: Essays in Canadian Literature and Poetics. First Choice Books: Victoria, 2015
Ploughing the Home Ground. QuodSermo Publishing, 2021
The View from Darien 2023

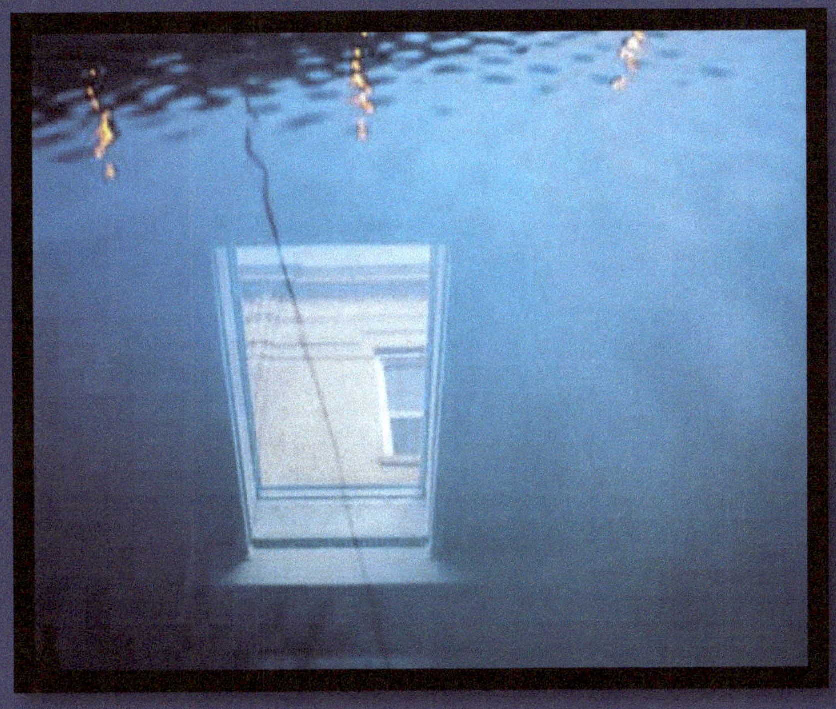

Robin Sutherland

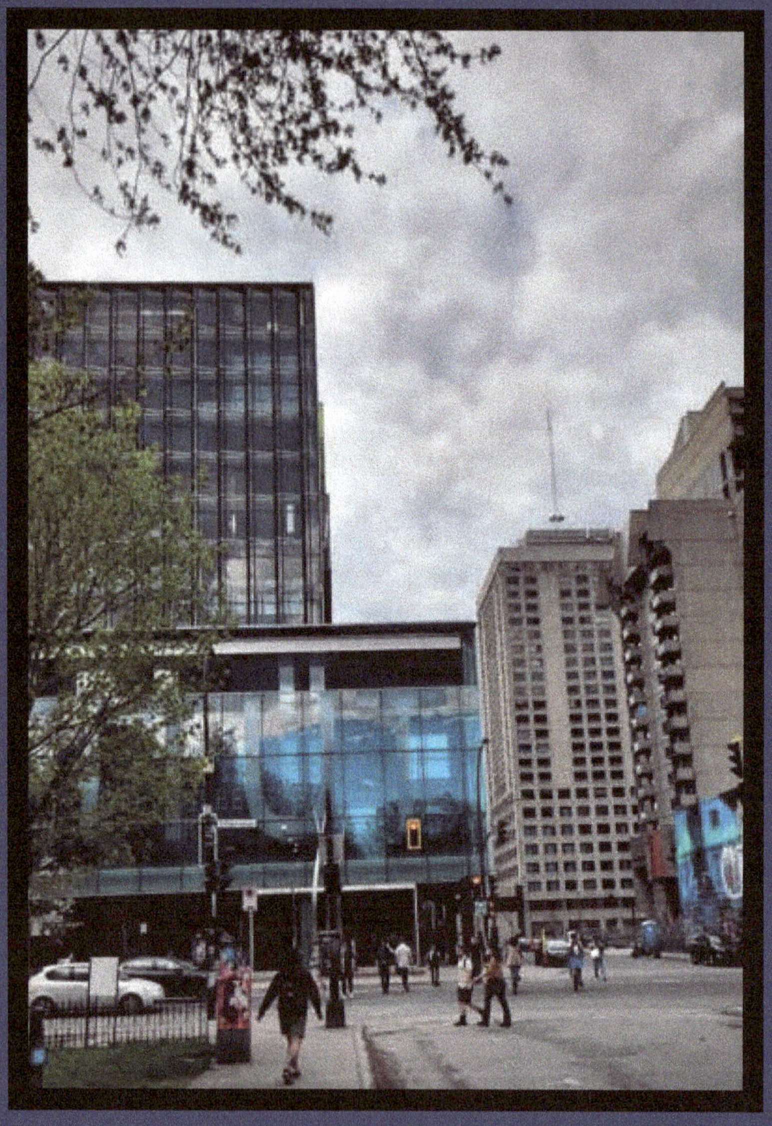

Anna Panunto
Montreal, Quebec

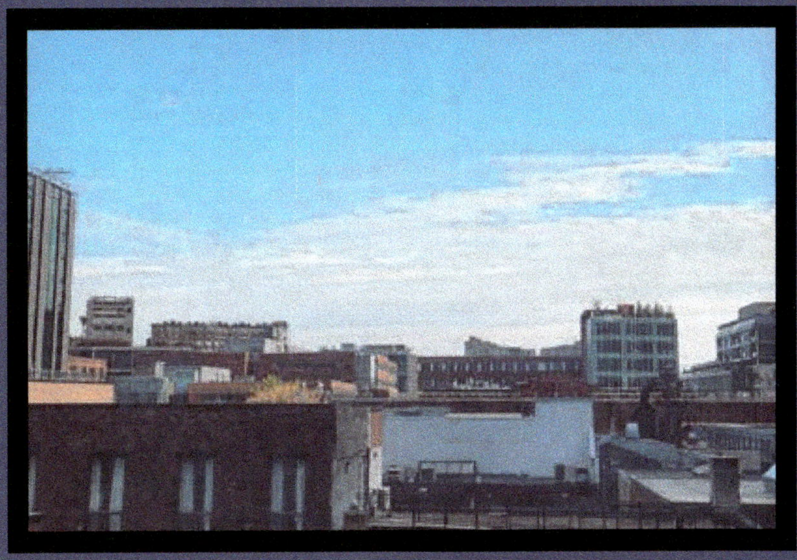

Anna Panunto
Montreal, Quebec

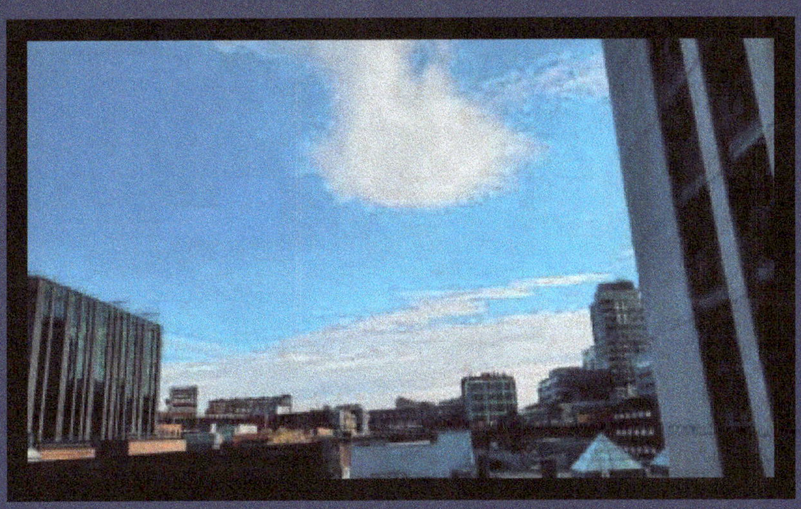

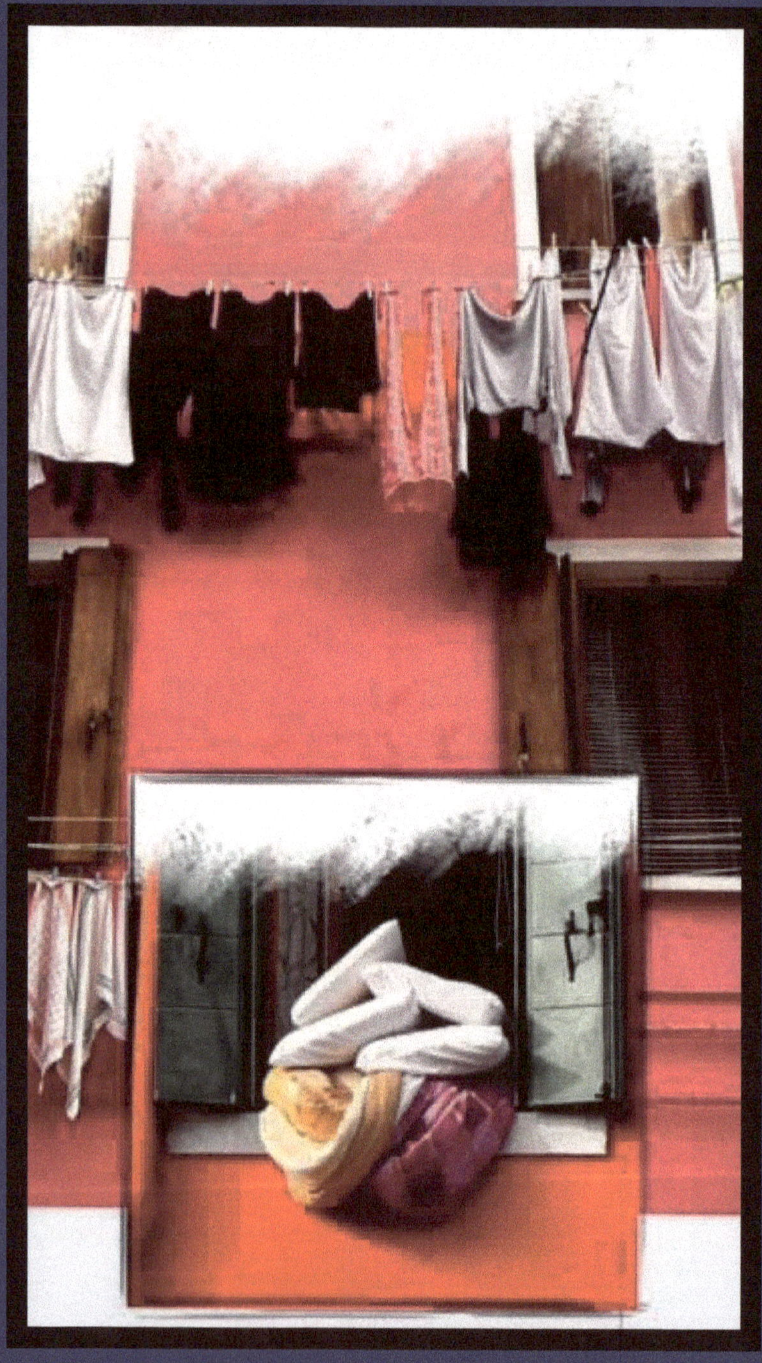

Ann Di Nardo
Pics of Venice 2023

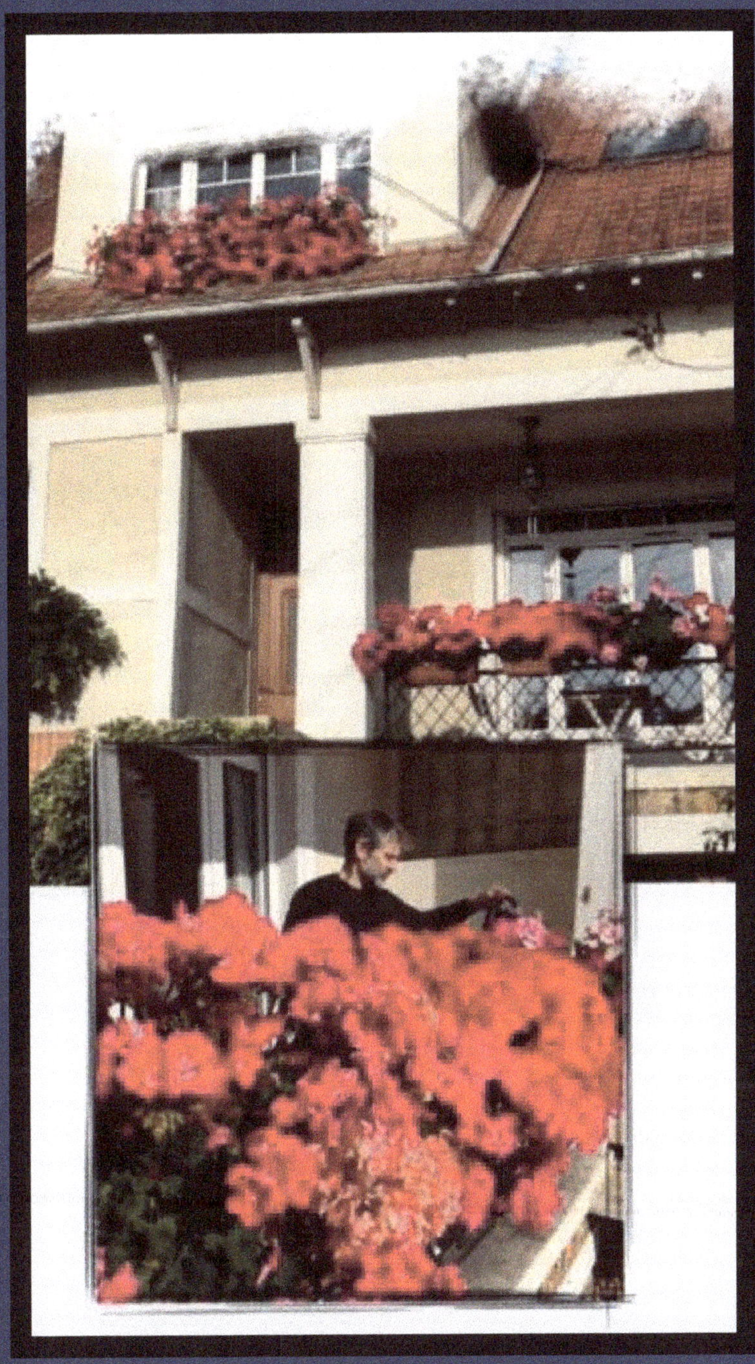

Ann Di Nardo
Pics of Venice 2023

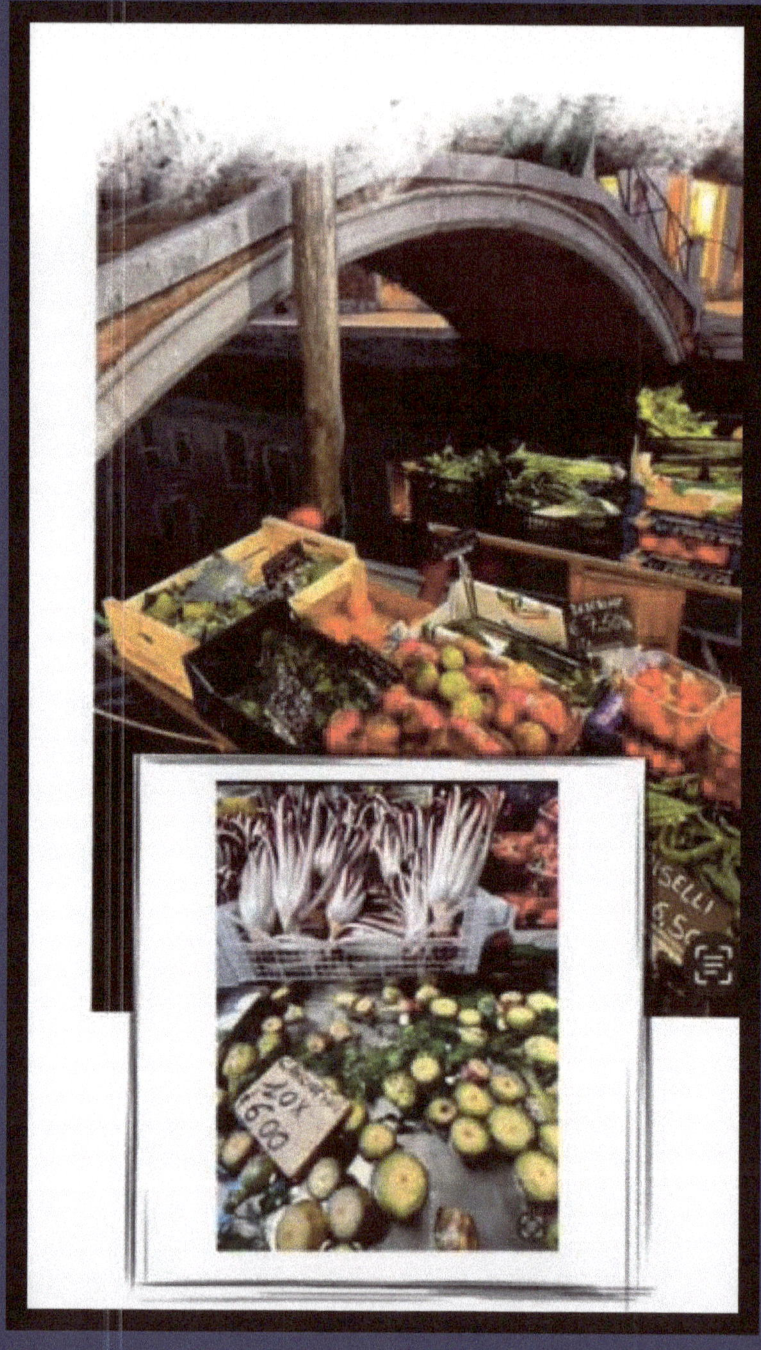

Ann Di Nardo
Pics of Venice 2023

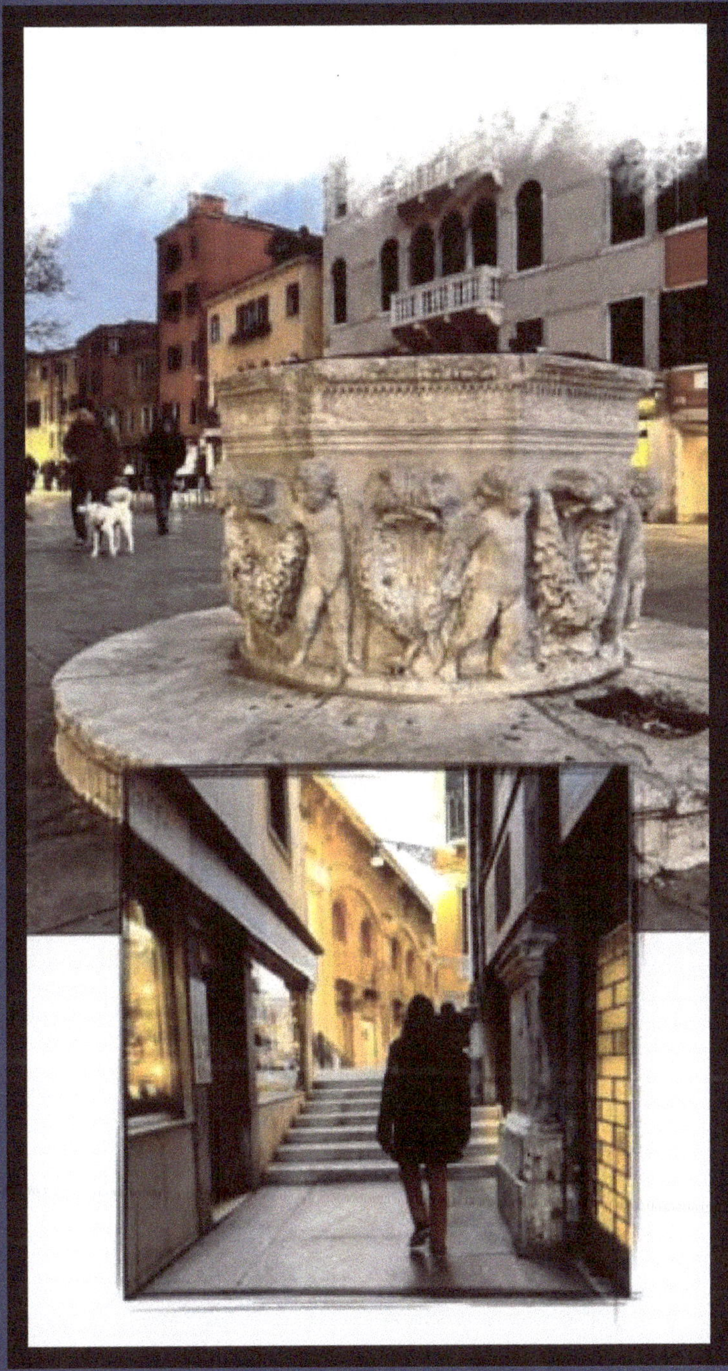

Ann Di Nardo
Pics of Venice 2023

Man is the loved of Love

For David

Dear Dear Roger and Veronica.
I am so so sad
to hear your news.
David's mind had simply been hijacked.
For him, very little
linked him to what we might call reality.
The two of you were likely
his primary link, his connection
to knowing anything about love.
He is now,
finally,
understanding
that he is the loved of Love.
Without body and drugs in his way,
he is finally seeing with clearly.
Nothing can take that away
from him now.
It is something that we will all
eventually understand
that we are
            the loved of Love.
I hope you all learn, sooner than later
that you are
            the loved of Love.
Know that for yourselves
and for dear David.
He was, is now and always will be
            the loved of Love.
That was, and is, and always will be
            his true identity.
Your love for David
is part of that eternal love.
He was blessed
to know it through you.

My love, the love of Love,
goes out to you both,
my dear friends.

Tai x

by Richard Marvin Tiberius (Tai) Grove

From the Christian Science Hymnal
#406 the last Stanza

O joy that ever will remain,
Midst seeming sorrow, hate, and pain,
Our hearts to fill with this glad song
That soars above the mists of wrong:
Man is the loved of Love.

Link to the full hymn — https://www.christianscience.com/additional-resources/churches-societies-and-groups/resources-for-hybrid-services-and-activities/music-for-branch-church-services/hymns-400-499

Scan QR Code —

www.ingramcontent.com/pod-product-compliance
Lightning Source LLC
Chambersburg PA
CBHW050031040726
47599CB00015B/1635